INTRENCHING AN OUTPOST.

PRACTICAL TREATISE

ON

STRENGTHENING AND DEFENDING

OUTPOSTS,

VILLAGES, HOUSES, BRIDGES, &c.,

IN REFERENCE TO THE

DUTIES OF OFFICERS IN COMMAND OF PICQUETS,

AS LAID DOWN IN THE FIELD EXERCISE AND EVOLUTIONS OF THE ARMY.

By J. JEBB,

Lieut.-Colonel in the Corps of Royal Engineers.

THIRD EDITION.

The Naval & Military Press Ltd

Published by

The Naval & Military Press Ltd
Unit 5 Riverside, Brambleside
Bellbrook Industrial Estate
Uckfield, East Sussex
TN22 1QQ England

Tel: +44 (0)1825 749494

www.naval-military-press.com
www.nmarchive.com

In reprinting in facsimile from the original, any imperfections are inevitably reproduced and the quality may fall short of modern type and cartographic standards.

TO THE

SUBALTERNS

OF

THE BRITISH ARMY,

THIS LITTLE TREATISE,

DESIGNED TO ASSIST THEM IN THE ACQUIREMENT

OF A PRACTICAL KNOWLEDGE OF

AN IMPORTANT DUTY,

IS INSCRIBED BY

A BROTHER OFFICER

PREFACE.

At page 302 of the King's Regulations for the Field Exercise and Evolutions of the Army,* it is laid down under the head of the "Duty of an Officer on Picquet," that his first care "ought to be the Strengthening of his Post " by constructing Abattis, Breastworks, &c., and especially when the Defence " of a Bridge or Ford is intrusted to him, he ought never to omit to throw " up something of the kind to protect his Men, and impede the advance of " an Enemy."

This Duty is further enforced in a stronger manner at page 317, where it is urged that " the Defence of the Posts should constitute a most im- " portant branch of every Officer's study, for upon Service all are liable to " be detached and placed in charge of Posts, with orders to defend them ;" and it is added, " In almost every case of this description, some measures " must be taken to protect the Party from being overcome by a Superior " Enemy ; while if placed to Guard a Bridge, or Watch a Ford, an Officer " who neglected to Strengthen his Post by every means in his power, and " to make the very most of his situation, would incur the hazard not only " of his own destruction, but of entailing some disaster on the Force from " which he was detached."

It is to be apprehended that few Young Officers give themselves the trouble to consider how these Orders are to be carried into effect, until they find themselves in some dangerous and critical situation in the Field, and the necessity arises for complying with them.

The following little Treatise is offered with a view of suggesting some Definite Ideas on the subject, and facilitating the Acquirement of a little Practical knowledge of a Duty which, from a long interval of Peace, and " the few opportunities that occur of giving Men and Officers any practical " Lessons in the Field," does not appear to excite that interest " in the " Service generally, which its importance deserves."

---

* This Treatise was first published in 1836, and the Regulations referred to are those which were in force at that time.

PREFACE.

My object has been, as far as possible, to discard all the Technicalities of Field Fortification, and not to enter further into the subject than merely to give a concise and familiar explanation of the nature and details of such TEMPORARY WORKS AS COULD BE COMPLETED IN A FEW HOURS, and for the construction of which, any Officer in charge of an Outpost would justly be held *Responsible*. In thus restricting myself, however, I have considered it desirable to enter more fully than is usual, into all the minor Details of Execution, and other arrangements for setting men to work; for unless these points are well understood, much valuable Time will of necessity be wasted before commencing Operations, and much confusion will probably attend the progress of them.

I do not claim to have originated anything new in these few pages, for the subject of which they treat has been written threadbare, by abler pens than mine: my only aim has been to condense a little Information into a Form that would be more easily got at, and understood, than where it is now to be found in volumes of Science, more immediately addressed to other branches of the Service, and generally mixed up with matter foreign to the purpose.

I was led, in the first instance, to commit a few memoranda to paper on this subject, after making a fruitless search for some Practical Work which had reference to Duties so pointedly enforced, without being Scientific, and which I was desirous of placing in the hands of a young Relative who had then just joined his Regiment: I have since been induced to add to, and arrange them in their present Form, and thus to make an attempt to supply the deficiency, in the sincere hope that a few pages, explanatory of these Duties, may prove useful to the Service.

J. J.

ROYAL ENGINEER ESTABLISHMENT, CHATHAM,
    8*th May*, 1836.

PREFACE TO THE SECOND EDITION.

IN preparing a Second Edition of this little Treatise within so short a period of its first publication, I have had the satisfaction of reflecting that the reception it has met with in the Military World, justifies the idea I had formed that some Work of the kind was wanted, and that it has been acceptable to the Service, in the form in which it appeared. I have therefore made but few alterations; but it is proposed to publish separately a Second Part, on the ATTACK OF MILITARY POSTS, which it is hoped, in conveying a familiar Explanation of that Subject, will also tend further to elucidate the corresponding measures of Defence, which are treated of in these pages.

CHATHAM,   J. J.
14*th June* 1837.

PREFACE TO THE THIRD EDITION.

THE object of the following pages has already been sufficiently explained. "An enlightened Public," having called for another edition, I again put myself at their mercy. In doing so, I would gladly have endeavoured to revise the whole, and render it more worthy of the subject I have endeavoured to explain, but "my hand is out." The years that have passed have been devoted to civil duties, and have brought with them no increase of experience in the Defence of Out-posts. I therefore again commit this little Treatise, with all its pristine defects, into the hands of the Subalterns and Soldiers of the Army, for whom it was originally written.

                                                                           J. JEBB,
                                                            Lieut.-Colonel Royal Engineers.

LONDON,
16*th March*, 1848.

CONTENTS.

Chapter I.

GENERAL RULES and PRINCIPLES which regulate Defensive Works—Flank Defence, how obtained in an Intrenched Position—Application of the same Principle in Strengthening a Town or Village—How applied in a Detached Post—Necessity of securing the Flanks enforced—Clearing Obstructions when they interfere with the Defence—Advantages of good Communications—Creating Obstructions—Observations on the Profile of Temporary Works—Disadvantages of Ground that is commanded, &c. 4

Chapter II.

PARTICULAR CONSIDERATIONS which influence the selection of a Military Post—Circumstances under which Outposts require to be strengthened—Description of Posts classed under three heads—Points requiring attention in the selection of the Post—The facilities it offers for being rendered Defensible—Nature of the Materials on the Spot, and the Soil—Its general Situation and Figure—The Object it is expected to fulfil—Its Distance from the Enemy—Number of Men for its Defence, and for Work—The Time there is to devote to it, &c. . . 9

Chapter III.

DETAILS OF EXECUTING BREASTWORKS, TRENCHES, &c.—Description of Tools and Stores required for the purpose—Proportions of each under different circumstances—Value of Sandbags—Division of Labour—Employment of Inhabitants—Average Work of an ordinary Labourer—Distribution of the Men—Proportionate Cover that may be obtained in a *given time*, and Remarks on the Form in which to arrange the Profiles, so as to secure all the advantages—Double manning Breastworks—Width of Ditches—Considerations on regulating the Profiles of Works—Communications through Breastworks, &c. . . 14

Chapter IV.

DEFENCE OF HEDGES, WALLS, WOODS, &c., illustrated by Sketches of various expedients and modes of rendering them available for purposes of Defence—Principles on which Loop-holes should be constructed, and mode of executing them—Tools to be used—How to secure the Defenders of a Wall from Artillery Fire—STOCKADE WORK, different modes of constructing it—How to render a Wood or Copse defensible 28

Chapter V.

OBSTRUCTIONS, essential to a vigorous Defence—AN ABATTIS, and mode of making it—PALISADES AND CHEVEAUX DE FRISE—their general dimensions, and the best way of fixing them—TRAP HOLES, and other temporary Expedients—Time of executing the above, and distribution of the Workmen—Collecting Materials, and the description that will be most useful, &c. 36

viii   CONTENTS.

Chapter VI.
                                                                   Page
OF PLACING BUILDINGS IN A STATE OF DEFENCE.—Different circumstances under which they may be required, and corresponding measures—Chief points to be looked to in selecting the Post—Considerations as to size—Mode of estimating the number of men proper for the Defence—Details of the various Works to be executed in the order of their relative importance—Collecting Materials—Barricading Doors and Windows—Levelling Obstructions—Making Ditches in front of the Doors, &c.—Cutting Loop-holes—Making Communications—Placing Abattis, &c—Constructing Tambours—Defence of the Outbuildings, &c. 42

Chapter VII.
OF PLACING A VILLAGE IN A STATE OF DEFENCE.—General Requisites it should possess as to its position, the nature and disposition of the Buildings, Extent, &c.—Circumstances under which it may require to be Intrenched—Measures to be pursued for obtaining immediate Security—Modes of applying the General Principles of Defence in the taking advantage of Local Objects—Barricades, Obstructions, &c.—Difference in the measures which require to be pursued *outside* and *inside* the Post, with reference to clearing away existing Obstructions—Importance of such Posts—Selection of the Keep, &c. 56

Chapter VIII.
ARRANGEMENTS FOR THE DEFENCE OF A BRIDGE.—Importance of a successful Defence—Circumstances that will influence the general Plan and mode of proceeding—Example and detail of laying out and executing Works for the Defence of a Bridge—Watching a Ford, mode of disputing the Passage, &c.   66

Chapter IX.
DEFENCE OF AN INTRENCHMENT.—General Dispositions to be made—In what respects it differs from the ordinary routine of Service in the Field—Necessity of having Support, and instilling Confidence—Disposition of the Force, and position of the Artillery—Precautions to be observed—Changes in the Dispositions, when the Attack becomes defined—Qualifications required in those who have to defend a Parapet—Comparison with the fights of "the olden times," &c. 76

Chapter X.
GUARDING AND DEFENDING A HOUSE.—General Dispositions to be made, and requisite Explanations—Use of Rockets and Grenades—Defence of Loop-holes—Guard on the Doors—Reserve—Communications—Retreat to the Upper Stories, and Defence—What measures of the Assailants should be regarded as "*Notice to quit*". 83

Chapter XI.
GUARDING AND DEFENDING AN INTRENCHED VILLAGE.—To avoid a Surprise, and to repel an Attack, shown to be the mainspring of all Defensive measures—Precautions and arrangements for securing them—Objects to be attained, and Evils to be avoided in seeking them—Distribution of the Forces and their Quarters—Commanding Officers to have ready means of communicating Orders to all their Detachments—Sorties—Retreats—Defence of the Keep, &c. 86

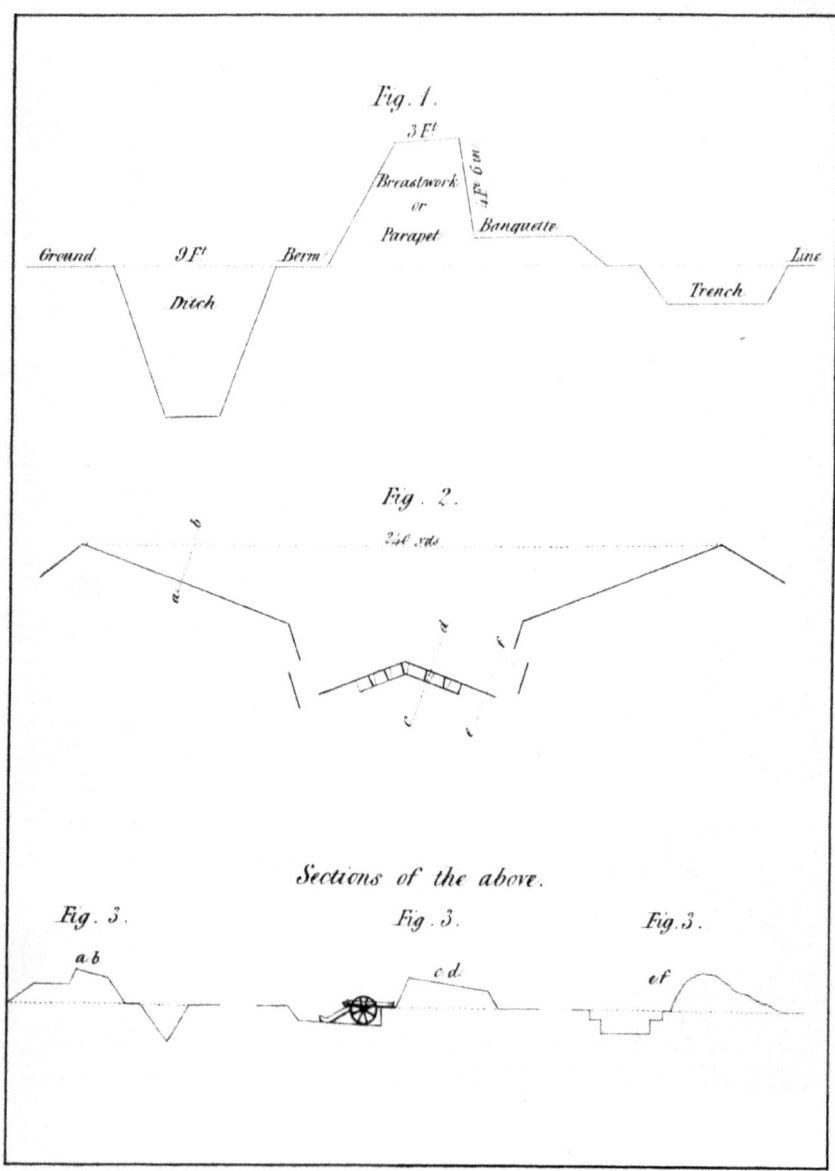

ON THE DEFENCE OF OUTPOSTS.

Definitions, &c.

1. The object of all Defensive Works, is to place a small Force under such advantages of situation, as to be able to cope with a larger one.

2. An Intrenchment may be said to be any continued Obstacle, from behind which Men may Defend themselves with comparative safety; or which keeps an Enemy at a distance from them; and it may be of two kinds; NATURAL or ARTIFICIAL.

A Natural Intrenchment may be a steep Bank, a Fence, a River, or a Marsh, &c., if they fulfil the above conditions.

An Artificial Intrenchment usually consists of a bank of earth called a Breastwork or Parapet, formed out of a Ditch, dug in front or rear of it.

The Figure and Extent of an Intrenchment,—the Thickness, Height, and Description of its Covering mass or Breastwork,—and the Breadth and Depth of its Ditch, depends entirely on circumstances to be hereafter explained.

3. A Breastwork or Parapet is the Covering mass of an Intrenchment, and it may also be Natural or Artificial; its use is to screen and protect the Defenders from the Missiles of an Enemy, and enable them to give their Fire in comparative security. Fig. 1.

To effect these objects it should be 6 or 7 feet high, so as to give Cover to a Man when standing upright, and there should be a step, usually called a BANQUETTE, on which he can stand, to Fire over the top of it with convenience.

The Thickness of a Breastwork must be proportioned to the Missiles it is intended to resist. Thus, from 7 to 8 feet of Earth will resist round shot from Field Artillery, and 1 foot of Earth or 6 inches of Timber, on an average, will be Musket-proof.

4. The PROFILE or VERTICAL SECTION of a Breastwork or Parapet, by which is meant its Thickness and Height, and the Slopes it may have to the Front and Rear, may be of any form, varying of course with circumstances of Ground and Situation, and the Materials it is made of. FIG. 1.

5. A TRENCH. Any little Ditch made *behind* a Breastwork, for Men to stand in for Cover, may be called a Trench, to distinguish it from a DITCH placed in *front* of a Breastwork, as an Obstacle to an Enemy. In either case the Excavation may furnish the earth for the Breastwork or Parapet if required. FIG. 1.

6. A BANQUETTE is a step on which Men stand to Fire over the top of a Breastwork or Parapet; it should generally be placed about 4 feet 6 inches below the top, which has been found a convenient average height for that purpose. FIG. 1.

7. A BERM. To prevent the Earth of which a Parapet or Breastwork is formed, from falling into the Ditch, a small space one or two feet broad is left between them, which is called a BERM. FIG. 1.

DEFINITIONS.

8. STOCKADE WORK, is rough substantial close Palisading, furnished with Loop-holes, and a Step or Banquette to Fire from. FIGS. 35 to 40.

9. An ABATTIS, is an Obstacle formed by felling a number of Trees, and laying them side by side, with the Branches well pointed and turned towards the Enemy; but in Woods, Copses, or Shrubberies, these forms may be dispensed with, and a very effective Abattis may be made by felling the Trees and Brushwood in all directions, so as to encumber the ground as much as possible.

10. A LOOP-HOLE is any opening which is made or arranged for Firing through with a Musket. No. 68. FIGS. 29 to 34.

11. A TRAVERSE. Any Mass which is interposed to protect men from Fire, which comes in any direction except their Front, is called a TRAVERSE. No. 132.

CHAP. I.—GENERAL RULES AND PRINCIPLES.

12. In all Fortification, whether of a Permanent or Temporary nature, each Line as far as is practicable should be seen and protected by another, within the effective range of Musketry or Artillery, according to the arm that is to be used for its Defence; and these Lines are best disposed when they stand Perpendicularly to each other, which is the direction that men generally fire in. It will be obvious, that when two Lines are so placed, if one of them should be attacked the Assailants would be exposed in Flank to the Fire of the other. This is what is meant by FLANK DEFENCE, or by one line being so situated as to FLANK another.

Thus in an Intrenched Position of any extent, Guns would be placed on the most advantageous points in the general line of the Works, and in the intervals between them, Lines for Musketry would be so disposed as to FLANK EACH OTHER, and to afford a CROSS FIRE over the ground in their Front. FIG. 2.

13. The same Principle applied in arranging Defensive Works in a Town or Village, would lead to the occupation of several Houses standing at right angles with each other, and to the construction of Breastworks across the Streets, or in such situations as would give a FLANKING FIRE along the front of those Houses, which were not seen one from the other in that direction.

14. Applied to the Defence of an isolated Country House or Farm, the relative position of the Outhouses,

GENERAL RULES AND PRINCIPLES.   5

Stables, and Garden walls would be studied, and if they did not afford Flank Defence for each other, it would be sought in the construction of some Temporary Work of a nature to be hereafter explained.

15. The same Principle may obviously be applied in Broken Ground, or in a Country intersected with Fences; the general contour and features of the former, and the general directions of the latter, one with another, would determine the Plan of Operations in reference to it.

16. In an Intrenched Line or Position, not inclosed in the rear, the situation and security of the FLANKS or extremities of the Line is a most important point; for they are more liable to be turned by a judicious Attack than those of an Army, without the advantage of being moveable.

Should they of necessity be Open and Unprotected, it might be desirable to have them rather retired, or to have a Second Line, so that if an Enemy made a serious attempt to turn either Flank of the Position, the Defenders of that portion of the Outer Line might receive more effective Support during an Attack, and have a Rallying Point to fall back upon, to prolong the resistance.

17. All Parts of a Line of Works should be EQUALLY STRONG, and where Nature or Local Circumstances have withheld their aid, Obstructions should be multiplied so as to compensate the weakness. The situations most exposed to Attack, should also be made more difficult of access, so as to equalize the whole Defence.

18. The ground within range of all Works should be as clear of Obstructions as the nature of circumstances

permit, so that an Enemy shall find no Cover, and be perfectly exposed when he approaches.

Thus in a Town or Village, the Houses in front of the situations occupied, if not levelled or set fire to, should be unroofed, the Parapet walls thrown down, and all Doors and Shutters removed. In an enclosed Country free from Buildings, the levelling of Fences, and filling in of Ditches, is perhaps all that could be attempted.

19. The surface of all Slopes should be seen, to the very foot of them if possible, and if within the extreme range of Musketry, be either laid under a FLANKING or DIRECT FIRE, as most convenient. An Enemy might otherwise advance and form under Cover at a moderate distance from a Work, which would favour the Attack, and enable him to support it. It may also be remarked, that as the Attack of an Intrenched Line is generally made in Columns, a Flanking fire, if it is near enough, is to be preferred to a Direct fire.

20. There should be well defined and well understood COMMUNICATIONS along the whole line of Works, of whatever nature they may be, so that if pressed in any particular point, a proportion of the distributed Force may readily be assembled there; and they should be so arranged as to be *shorter* than those by which the Enemy could alter his dispositions during the Attack. If the Line is extensive, the means of Retreat from each portion of it to some central point in the Rear, should not be overlooked, as it will give increased confidence to the Defenders, and enable them to stand their ground to the last moment; and in Retreat, their local knowledge will give them immense

GENERAL RULES AND PRINCIPLES.   7

advantages, in disputing the advance of a hostile Force. See FIG. 53.

"On fait d'autant mieux la Guerre defensive que l'on connait mieux le pays."

21. It is very essential to create OBSTRUCTIONS within the short range of Musketry, in front of all Works of a Temporary nature, with a view of breaking the order of the Assailants, and detaining them under a close and severe fire, if they persist in forcing their way through. In fact all the movements of an Enemy, whether to the front, right, or left, should be as much cramped and impeded as possible. It is half the battle to break his order or put him in confusion when under fire, for he can seldom reform under such circumstances, and if he attacks in disorder, the chances are against his success.

22. It is very desirable that the PROFILE, or form of such Temporary Works as of themselves offer no Impediment to the advance of an Enemy, should be so regulated, that whilst they provide effectual Cover for the Defenders, they should afford as little as possible to an Attacking Force should they be taken, but should leave it exposed to the Fire of the Reserve, and liable to be attacked in return, and driven out again. FIG. 6 compared with FIG. 7, will illustrate this remark. In the former it will be observed that 6 feet of Cover is obtained for Defenders standing in the Trench, whilst an Enemy who might succeed in driving them out, would only derive a Cover of 3 feet, by sheltering himself on the *outside* of the Parapet. In the latter Figure there is equal Cover on both sides.

23. GROUND THAT IS COMMANDED BY HEIGHTS on the Front or Flanks, within range of Field Artillery, should

always be avoided in selecting a position for an Intrenchment, unless it is defiladed by nature. The inconvenience arising from a command in Front may be partially obviated by deepening the Trenches, and thus obtaining proportionate Cover; but if Heights are domineering over the Flanks, and an Enemy can have access to them, the different lines of Breastwork would be exposed to a dangerous Plunging Fire in the direction of their length, which might render them untenable. A partial Enfilade, or Flank Fire, may be obviated by the erection of Traverses, here and there, as required. No. 11.

Chap. II.—Particular Considerations.

24. THE CIRCUMSTANCES UNDER WHICH OUTPOSTS REQUIRE TO BE STRENGTHENED in the temporary manner under discussion are infinite, and it would be out of place in a little Treatise of this description, to attempt anything like a detail of them.

The kind of Posts also which may be occupied, vary in a greater degree than the circumstances; depending on the construction and disposition of the Buildings and Fences, and the Inequalities of the ground on which they are situated; defined instructions cannot therefore be laid down which will apply in all cases, but 'WHERE RULES END, GENIUS BEGINS.' Such Posts too, require to be strengthened on the spur of the moment, and almost in the presence of an Enemy, where there is no time for deliberation, and it may be, when he who 'hesitates is lost.'

25 It needs no argument therefore to show, that an Officer who has no further Ambition than being merely prepared for the proper discharge of an acknowledged Duty, should embrace any opportunity that offers, (and every walk he takes will afford him one,) of examining and endeavouring to appreciate the advantages that may be taken of the ever-varying circumstances of Ground or Position; and that he should also make himself thoroughly acquainted with the most approved and simple Expedients for turning them to the best account.

Some individuals may possess greater facility than others, in acquiring a habit of determining at a glance what is the most judicious mode of disposing a Force, and arranging Defensive Works for strengthening a Post; but a very little time devoted to the study of the subject, would render any one competent to decide upon it to the extent of the responsibility devolving upon an Officer in command of a Piquet, or charged with the Defence of an Outpost.

26. But to return to the subject: the description of Posts under discussion, naturally fall under three heads, viz.—

First. Such as require to be ARTIFICIALLY CREATED by the construction of all the Works that are requisite for protection and defence.

Second. Such as from favorable circumstances of ground, &c. only require to have EXISTING OBJECTS IMPROVED UPON, to be equally defensible.

Third. And which is the most common, A UNION OF THESE TWO.

27. THE SELECTION OF THE POST where a choice is admitted, is what will first engage attention, and the following considerations must have their weight in determining the point.

28. The Inequalities of the Ground, and the Objects upon it, such as Buildings or Fences, &c., should be of such a nature, and in that relative situation to each other, as to be convertible into a Fortified Post with THE LEAST POSSIBLE LABOUR, AND IN THE SHORTEST TIME.

29. The Position should not be commanded, especially on the Flanks or in the Rear, within the ordinary range of a Field Piece. No. 23.

30. There should be plenty of Materials on the spot for the construction of Temporary Works, and for forming Obstructions in front of them.

PARTICULAR CONSIDERATIONS. 11

31. The Soil should be of a nature that is easily worked, if it is foreseen that any Trenches or Ditches will have to be executed.

32. It should generally be DIFFICULT OF ACCESS, and yet offer the MEANS OF RETREATING in security.

33. And should be in a situation for fulfilling the object for which the Detachment is to be posted.

34. In arranging the General Plan for occupying it with Defensive Works, the following points among others will require more particular attention.

35. It must be ascertained from a minute examination of the Position, what Figure of a Work will suit it, so that the greatest quantity of Fire may be directed over the most accessible points of attack, and that the general contour of the Intrenchment may fall in with the Ground, and the Buildings or Fences that are upon it.

36. THE OBJECT THE WORK IS EXPECTED TO FULFIL in reference to the Force with which it is in connexion; the Distance it is removed from that Force; whether instant support may be expected, or whether it is to be left to itself to hold an Enemy in Check as long as possible; or whether it is to be defended to the last extremity.

37. ITS SITUATION WITH RESPECT TO THE ENEMY as to Distance, &c.; whether it is likely to be attacked by overwhelming Forces, or only subject to the brusque attack of Cavalry or Infantry in smaller bodies; whether Artillery is likely to be brought up against it, for in that case Earthen Works, when merely for the purposes of Cover, are in some respects better than Buildings, or Stockades; the Parapets, too, must be thicker;—whether it can be

surrounded, for in such a case it must be enclosed all round, &c.

38. THE NUMBER OF MEN THERE WILL BE FOR ITS DEFENCE, taking it as an Established rule, that it is better to have a Force concentrated, than too much distributed, and therefore injudicious to make Works of a greater extent than can be well manned and vigorously defended.

"Celui qui partagera ses forces sera battu en detail."

For instance, in small Works there might be a File of men for every Pace or Yard in the length of their Breastwork, and in larger ones the same, with a Reserve of from one-fourth to one-sixth of the whole in addition. On some such general basis, a calculation of the Proportionate Extent of a Work might be made. All this of course depending very much upon circumstances.

39. THE NUMBER OF MEN, whether Soldiers or Inhabitants, that can be collected together for working, and whether there are Tools enough for them, so as not to undertake more work than can be well done.

40. And which is a very important point, THE TIME THERE IS TO DO IT IN. Whether an immediate Attack is to be apprehended, or otherwise, for this will decide not only the nature of the Works, but the parts of them that require the first attention; as will be more apparent when the Details of Execution are brought under consideration.

41. THE NATURE OF THE MATERIALS that can be had on the spot, or procured in the neighbourhood. This will have a great influence on the Details of the plan to be pursued, and will afford opportunity for the display of considerable tact and intelligence, in appropriating and

adapting the means at hand for carrying the general plan into effect, and securing its objects with the LEAST POSSIBLE LABOUR.

42. No one who is not conversant with work of this description, can have an idea of the great saving of Time and Labour that may be effected, by taking advantage of what might appear at a casual glance to be very unimportant local features; such, for instance, as gentle undulations in the ground.

A reference to FIG. 16 will illustrate this remark, in showing the obvious difference of labour in obtaining the same amount of Cover on different sides of a Slope.

Chap. III.—Details of Execution.

43. The following description of Tools and Stores would be found more or less necessary, where Temporary Works were to be thrown up, and they should be furnished in the required proportions to any Detachment whose duty it might be to strengthen and afterwards defend a Post.

44. They are classed in three Divisions, that their separate uses may be apparent.

Class 1. Field Exercise Tools.

Shovels, Pickaxes, Felling-axes, Bill-hooks, — For sinking Trenches, forming Breastworks, felling Timber, making Abattis and Obstructions, &c.

Class 2. For Houses, Walls, &c.

Sledge-hammers, Hand-borers, Crow-bars, Saws, Augurs, Spike nails, — For forming Loop-holes, breaking through Walls, preparing timber for Barricades, Stockade work, &c.

Class 3. General Service and purposes of Defence.

Sand-bags, Rockets, Small shells, Hand grenades, — The Sand-bags for blocking up Windows, and forming Loop-holes, &c. The Rockets and Shells for defence of Houses and Intrenchments.

DETAILS OF EXECUTION. 15

45. The proportions of these necessary to be demanded would of course vary with the Description of work which might be anticipated.

For example, in throwing up Earthen Works in an Open country, a Pickaxe and Shovel for every man that could be employed on the Breastworks would be wanted. If an Abattis could be formed, and there were Fences to be cut up and levelled, one third of the Men would be advantageously employed with Felling-axes and Bill-hooks. In a case where Houses were to be placed in a state of defence, Walls would have to be broken through for making Loop-holes, and Windows, Doors and Passages to be barricaded; here Crow-bars, Hand-borers, Sledge-hammers, Spike nails, and Saws would be required in greater proportion than Spades and Pickaxes.

Sand-bags are included as being very useful for many purposes, such as protecting men when firing over a Parapet or Breastwork; quickly blocking up the lower parts of Windows, &c. In each case, Loop-holes being arranged by disposing them as shown in FIG. 34.

A man will carry one hundred empty Sand-bags, weighing about 60 lbs, each of which will contain a Bushel of earth, and when *full* they are *Musket proof.* Don't forget that.

Rockets,* small Shells, and Grenades, are mentioned as

---

* As an illustration of the use of Rockets, it may be mentioned that on one occasion during the late war in Canada, an American Gun boat took up a position which enfiladed a situation where a Bridge that had been destroyed was being re-established; from whence she kept up a fire that bid fair to stop proceedings. Artillery could not be brought up, but luckily Rockets were thought of, and a few were obtained from the rear. The second that was fired entered her bows, and caused so many casualties,

being very powerful and attainable auxiliaries in the defence of Posts and Houses; and one great advantage of them is, that any body who has common sense may use them, or at least be instructed in the requisite precautions in a few minutes.

46. A certain DIVISION OF LABOUR must also be attended to, and a man should always have a Tool put into his hand that he has been accustomed to use; Carpenters should therefore be employed where Saws and Axes are wanted; Miners and Blacksmiths where Walls are to be broken through; Laborers where the Spade and Pickaxe come into play. Those who never handled Tools of these descriptions, would be most usefully employed in collecting Materials. It would be well also to select such men for the first tour of duty, as Patrols, and Sentries, and to employ the best workmen in overcoming the greatest difficulties, which are usually found in the commencement. A little foresight will not be misapplied in considering these points.

47. It is essential to obtain the assistance of the Inhabitants in executing Works of this description, and an Officer should always have authority to enforce their attendance, and to pay them in proportion to their exertions. They should also be required to bring with them whatever Tools they can best use, or that are most wanted.

---

that the 24-pounder was reduced to silence; and it was only by a shift of wind that the boat was got off, after being driven close in shore, and many of the remaining men being killed or wounded by a light company that ran into the water up to their pouches, in the hopes of taking her.

PLATE. II.

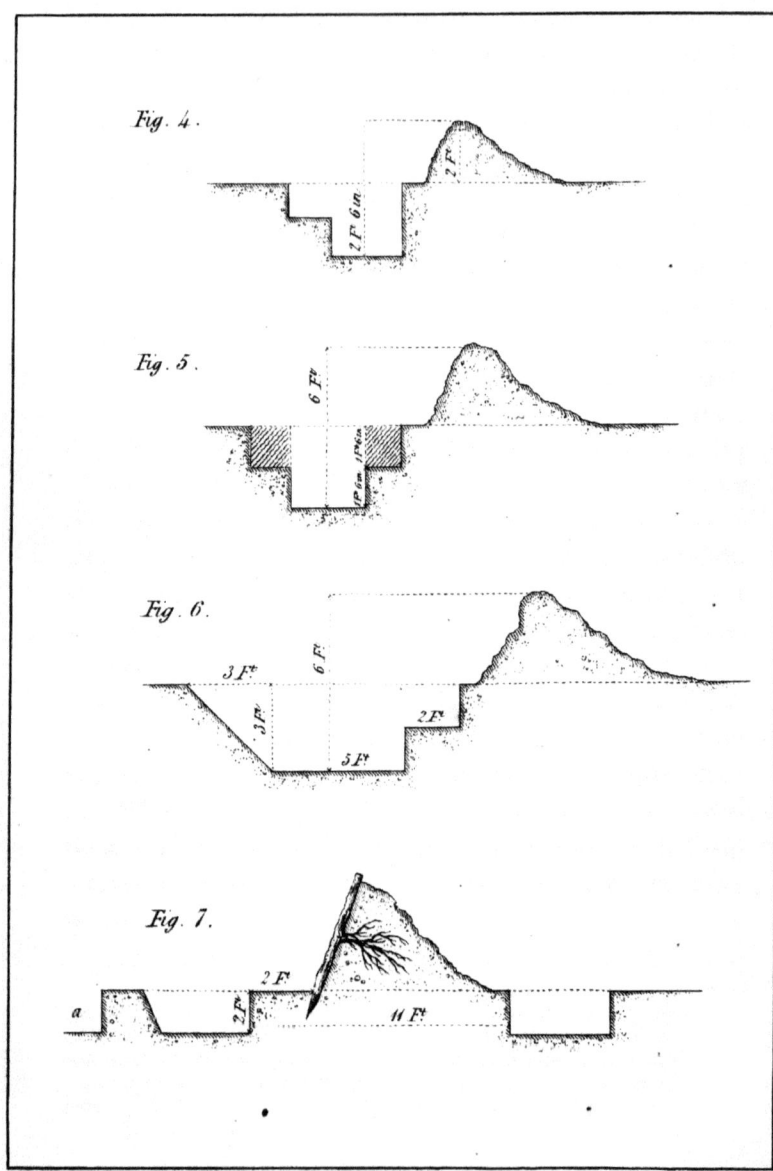

BREASTWORKS.

48. Under the first consideration, adverted to in No. 26, that whatever is required for Protection and Defence, has to be ARTIFICIALLY CREATED.

A general idea may be formed of the Quantity of work that can be done in a Given Time, and of the proportion of Cover that may be obtained in that time, by adopting different Sections when throwing up the earth, on referring to the annexed Figures 4 to 8, and the corresponding Estimates, which are calculated on the following Data.

First. That on an average, an Ordinary Labourer will dig out 1 CUBIC YARD OR 27 CUBIC FEET OF EARTH, AN HOUR, in middling soil; and continue to work at that rate for eight hours or more. And secondly, on the supposition that EACH MAN HAS 6 FEET IN LENGTH TO EXECUTE, which distance enables him, when at work with others in a line, to use his Tools with perfect freedom.

It should be observed that the First of these Data admits of considerable latitude, and A CUBIC YARD AN HOUR, which is a convenient average to remember, is the least work that ought to be expected, unless in a very strong hard soil; in a light sand not requiring much use of the Pickaxe, an indifferent Labourer would remove 2 Cubic yards an Hour with more facility than he would 1, in Difficult soil; and bearing this in mind, the nature of the soil on which a Military Post might be situated, would frequently have a great influence in modifying the details. With regard to the supposed DISTANCE OF 6 FEET FOR EACH PORTION, it is not to be considered *invariable* but *convenient*. Men may be set to work as near as 4 feet from each other, but the

Time gained is not in proportion to the diminished Distance, for they will be too crowded to work with ease, and they will be liable to injure each other, especially at night. Still, however, there is no doubt that any given quantity of work would be completed in less time by disposing workmen at 4 or 4½ feet than at a greater distance. On the other hand, when only improving the Natural advantages offered by Banks, Fences, &c., the working parties might be distributed at much wider intervals than 6 feet: having reference to the Time in which they could execute any given portion. For instance, a man might possibly convert 20 or 30 feet of a Hedge into a good Breastwork in three hours, when he could not execute 6 feet in length, of one equally defensible, in the same time, that required to be artificially created on a Level Field. An Officer should never shackle his mind by precise rules; it should rather be his study to obtain a clear perception of *General Principles*, and of the immediate object he has in applying them. Book that!

49. Before entering further into the Details, it may be right to mention as a General Rule, that in almost all cases where Trenches are required, it is essential that the means of getting out of them with facility, both to the Front and Rear, should be preserved, by leaving Slopes or Steps for that purpose. Thus on some occasions it is desirable they should offer no impediment to a forward or a retrograde movement, but that Troops should be able to march straight over them when necessary. In the Trenches, however, which will now be brought more immediately under consideration, and which are designed not only to provide Cover, but to be vigorously Defended when attacked, the

chief object of making a Step in the rear would be, that the Defenders instead of waiting for the Assailants in the bottom of the Trench, might step out after giving their last fire, and thus interpose a fresh Obstacle between them and their enemy, besides placing themselves in a better attitude for resistance.

50. FIG. 4—in the annexed Plate, represents the Section of a small Trench, and the Parapet or Breastwork that has been formed by throwing the earth up in front of it. The Trench is $2\frac{1}{2}$ feet deep, and the same width, having a rough Step of 1 foot broad in the rear. The earth thrown out will make a Parapet of a height nearly equal to the depth of the Trench, without taking any precautions in building it up at a steeper Slope than it will stand at of itself; we will assume that it is 2 feet high, which will make a total of $4\frac{1}{2}$ feet from the bottom of the Trench. A man therefore, though he can reach to fire over the top of the Parapet, has to stoop to be wholly concealed or covered by it, and it therefore affords as little protection, as is worth the trouble of considering in this place.

The Solid Content of the excavation, from which the probable Time it will take to execute may be determined, is found by multiplying the Depth and Breadth of the Trench together, for the Superficial measure or Area of the Section, and that product by the Length each man has to do. Here $2\frac{1}{2}$ feet multiplied by $2\frac{1}{2}$ feet, is equal to $6\frac{1}{4}$ feet, and that product multiplied by 6 feet, which we have assumed to be the portion allotted to each workman, gives $37\frac{1}{2}$ cubic feet. The Step is 1 foot broad and 1 foot deep, and being 6 feet as before in length, there will be 6 solid feet more to add, making altogether $43\frac{1}{2}$ cubic feet for the Solid content of the mass of earth that has been removed.

Now if a man is only supposed to dig out 27 cubic feet in an Hour, it will take him rather more than an Hour and a half to remove 43½ cubic feet on level ground.

51. Fig. 5—affords more Cover, for the top of the Parapet is 6 feet above the bottom of the Trench. The best way of executing such a Profile would be to sink a Trench 3 feet deep and 3 feet wide, and to throw the earth about 2 feet in front of it; so that in the progress of the work, when the Trench was found to be too deep to stand in, and fire with convenience over the top of the Parapet, a little Step might be cut out of the solid left in front, for a Banquette, as shown shaded in the section; and another step of the same description in the rear would complete it as far as it went. The steps might be 18 inches wide, and the same depth.

The Area of this Section is nearly 14 feet, the Trench itself being 9 feet, and the two steps 4½ superficial measure, which multiplied by 6 feet, the length of the portion allotted to each workman as before, gives 84 Cubic feet, or about 3 Cubic yards, for the Solid content of the excavation; and therefore, under the presumed Data, it would be completed in three hours: still however it will be observed, that it offers no Impediment in itself to an Enemy, and men could only be drawn up in single file for its defence, from their not being room for more.

52. A Trench of the dimensions shown in Fig. 6 might be completed in five hours on the presumed Data, and being roomy enough to dispose Men in Double Files for its Defence, and high enough to Screen and Cover them, may be

considered as large as is necessary for merely fulfilling those conditions; for if more time could be devoted to strengthening a Post, or if other circumstances were favorable, it would become a consideration whether some Profile of a different form could not be substituted with advantage, for such as only afford Cover, without opposing any Obstacle to the advance of a hostile Force, as will be explained in No. 56.

53. FIG. 7—is a form of Breastwork that might be adopted for obtaining Cover in Rocky or Marshy situations, where a Ditch or Trench could not be made deeper than 1 or 2 feet; and if there were plenty of men they might be set to work in two lines, and get it completed in half the time it would otherwise take, either by sinking on each side of the proposed situation, or by arranging the men in two lines behind it, as shown in the Figure, where the Situation for the Second line of Workmen is shown at (a).

To work on both sides the Breastwork, which is the quickest way, it would have to be considered what breadth of ground the Breastwork with its Slopes to the front and rear would stand upon, and what breadth the Banquette and Berm ought to be. These particulars being determined, two parallel lines would be roughly traced on the ground with pickets, at the required distance. The workmen would be drawn up facing each other on these lines, and would work backwards, throwing the earth into the space between them, which some spare men would form into the Breastwork.

Here sinking only 2 feet, the Breastwork must be raised 4½ feet to obtain Cover. Suppose the Slope on the inside is made steep by building it up with Sods, or other Materials, so that it only occupies 18 inches of level ground, the Outside Slope, being left to find its own level, will require a Base equal to its height, or 4 feet 6 inches ; and if we add 2 feet for the thickness of the Breastwork at the top, it will cover 8 feet of ground. Then if the Banquette be made 2 feet broad, and the Berm 1 foot, the distance between the two lines of workmen will be altogether 11 feet.

Under the second supposition, if the two lines of workmen were drawn up one behind the other, and both working to the same front, the distance between them might be from 4 to 7 feet, according to the depth.

The level of the ground in this instance forms the Banquette or Step to fire from. There will be about 5 Cubic yards in 6 running feet of Breastwork, and as there are supposed to be a double number of Men at work, it ought to be finished in two or three hours.*

54. This mode of executing Work may also be adopted with advantage, in other cases when Time is an object, and there are plenty of hands, or when it is of importance to strengthen and give height to Breastworks in particular situations. But as far as this Profile is concerned, it is to be observed, that it would afford Cover to an Enemy when he got at it, without opposing any impediment to his advance, which it is always very desirable to avoid. (No. 22.)

55. Should the Ground be Rocky or very hard, as in a Road or Street, Cover may perhaps be more expeditiously obtained by raising a Breastwork from Rubbish or Materials

---

* When from circumstances the depth of a Trench or Ditch is very limited, the probable time it will take to form a Breastwork out of them, is more readily determined by estimating the content of the *mass* to be raised, than the *excavation*, as in the preceding cases, because the breadth of the latter will probably be irregular.

PLATE. III.

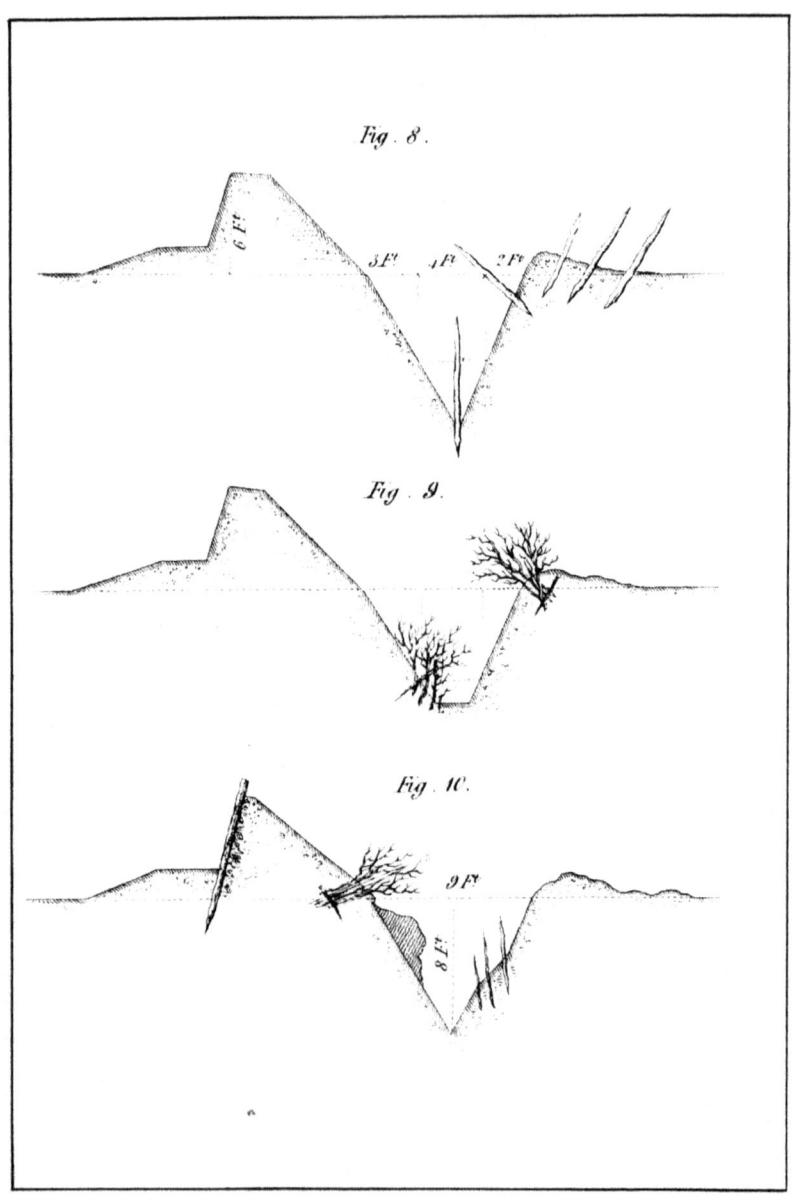

brought to the spot in Baskets, Sand-bags, or Barrows, than in attempting to sink at all. Different expedients are shown in FIGS. 14 and 15.

56. Having thus far detailed the most expeditious modes of providing Cover for men, it may now be worth while to consider whether in securing that advantage for the Defenders, you cannot at the same time add another, in opposing an *Obstacle* to an Enemy, by excavating a Ditch in *front* of the Breastwork in place of making a Trench in *rear* of it. A Ditch to stop people at all, should not be *jumpable*, either "flying," or "in and out," and it should therefore be at least 8 or 9 feet broad, and 6 or 8 feet deep; in more Permanent Works it would of course be considerably more.

57. FIG. 8—shows the general Dimensions which such a Profile might have. The Ditch it will be observed is of a triangular form, the Area of which, for calculating the quantity of earth to be moved, will be found by multiplying its Breadth by *one-half* its Depth, that is 9 feet by 4 feet, which gives 36 superficial feet; and that multiplied again by the Length of the portion each man has to execute, (we will here say 4 feet, as the Breadth is considerable) will be $36 \times 4 = 144$ Cubic feet, or about 5 Cubic yards in each portion of 4 feet; which, considering the increased labour arising from a greater depth than has hitherto been contemplated, would not probably be completed in less than 6 Hours by the same Workmen. Some spare men, probably equal to one-half the number employed in the Ditch, would also be required for ramming the Earth, and forming the Breastwork. Thus, on 100 feet in length there would be 25 Men working in the Ditch, and 12 additional, making

in all 37; whilst in the common Trench work, which has hitherto been under consideration, only about 17 Workmen have been shown to be necessary for every 100 feet.

58. A Profile, such as that now under discussion, therefore requires not only longer time to execute, but Double the number of Men; and it would not seem advisable to undertake it, unless there were a reasonable probability of its being completed before an Attack could be made; for if an Enemy came upon it when in an unfinished state, it would be almost useless, and the labour, which if otherwise applied would have secured at least good Cover, would thus be thrown away. Still, however, the advantages it offers should not be lost sight of in situations where a determined stand is to be made, and on very accessible points, or to shut up Roads or Streets, &c., even if the rest of an Intrenchment were differently arranged. As far as the means of Resistance is concerned, it is obviously of more advantage to have a Ditch in front of a Breastwork than a Trench in rear of one; and the only point to be determined is whether there is TIME and MEANS for executing it: and it is on this point that an Officer will have to exercise his discrimination, when he has carefully considered the various Circumstances of his situation, which will have influence upon it; and which have already been detailed in the Second Chapter.

59. Such a Profile may further be much strengthened by planting a row of Palisades in the Ditch, or even by driving Stakes in and sharpening them, or making what may be called a perpendicular Abattis, by planting Brushwood upright in the bottom, with the ends sharpened, as shown in FIGS. 8 and 9.

GENERAL OBSERVATIONS. 25

An expeditious way also of adding to the Difficulties of an Assault is shown in FIG. 10, where common Hurdles or Gates, Rails or Brushwood, laid on the ground soon after commencing the work, and their extremities buried under the Parapet, may be made use of: the earth underneath them, shaded dark in the Figure, should be cut away, when the Ditch has been sunk to its full depth.

Short Posts laid horizontally every 8 or 10 feet in the same situation, and long Rails or a Chain afterwards nailed to them, would be a ready expedient; the ends should project about 2 feet over the Ditch, and stand at least 6 feet above the bottom of it.

60. It is to be observed that in all the foregoing cases, only a MINIMUM OF COVER, AND MEANS OF RESISTANCE has been sought for, in a MINIMUM OF TIME. It has been shown WHAT CAN BE EFFECTED IN A FEW HOURS, "*faut de mieux;*" it may so happen however, that Time is given to improve upon the Profiles described, as would be the case if an Advanced Post were held for some days in succession, and each Officer in command had done what he could towards it. These Improvements would consist in strengthening the Breastworks, making the Ditches deeper and wider, and planting more redoubtable Obstructions; and such opportunities must never be thrown away, as the means of Defence, and the security afforded, will be augmented in proportion.

61. It may be remarked, that such Breastworks as offer little or no Impediment of themselves to an Enemy, if well laid out, permit the Defenders to charge over them in Line if they wish it, and still possess one of the principal attributes of any work, which is that of *screening them from*

previous Observation. But a forward Movement from those that do offer an Obstruction, must be through an Opening, and therefore on a narrow Front.

Now the space between a Breastwork and an Obstruction placed in Front of it, is ground belonging to the Defenders which, if circumstances permit, should be disputed; and as an Enemy would probably be in some confusion in forcing his way through such Obstruction, a favorable moment would doubtless occur for making a Sudden Charge, which, supported by a good Flank Fire, ought to be successful. These Advantages should never be lost sight of, in arranging the General Plan of Defensive Works, and determining the Profiles they shall have. A reference to Fig. 2, and the Sections belonging to it, Fig. 3, will illustrate these remarks. The Salient angles of the Intrenched Line are the points most open to attack, and it will be observed that the Profile of the Lines, terminating in those Salients, has a Ditch in front which presents more or less of an Obstacle; whilst the Profile of the Line adjoining the Battery in the centre, is only that of a Trench for providing Cover, because it is not in a situation open to attack.

Communications through Breastworks, &c.

62. When an Opening or Passage is required through a Breastwork or Stockade, it must be arranged so as to be easily closed and defended. These objects may be in some measure secured by disposing the Lines in such forms as are represented in Figs. 11 and 12, and providing rough strong Gates, Chevaux de frize, or something of the sort, for quickly shutting them up. When Houses are concerned,

PLATE. IV.

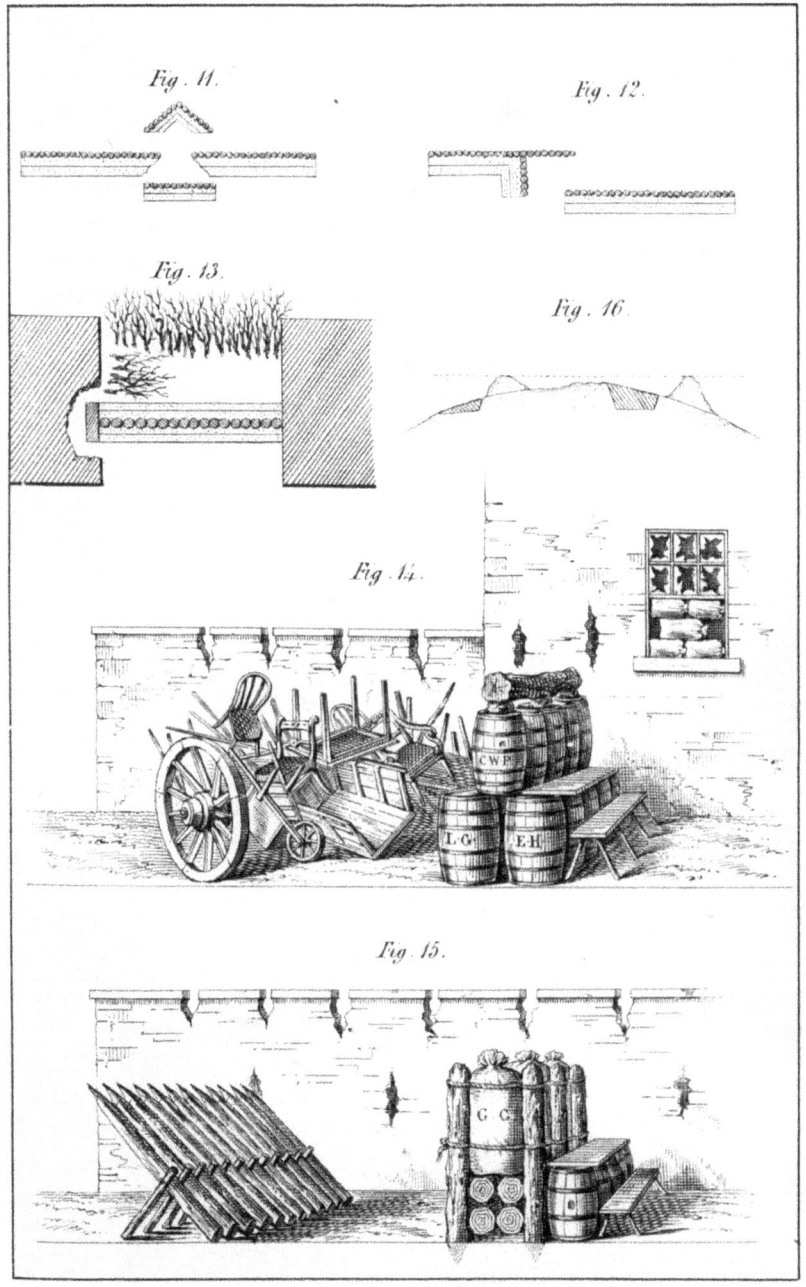

as in a Street, the Barricade may extend quite across, and a Communication be made round the end of it, by breaking through Walls, as shown in FIG. 13. It will be observed also in FIG. 53, which is the plan of a Village prepared for Defence, that the Houses bordering upon the Breastworks are completely cut through to secure the means of ready communication, the necessity of which was enforced in No. 20.

Chap. IV.—Defence of Hedges, Roads, &c.

63. In the foregoing explanation of the Details of Breastworks, an attempt has been made to show the least possible Time in which decent Cover could be obtained when working on a level plain unaided by any advantages of Ground and Situation; and it must be confessed it is rather a damper to one's ardour to find, that five or six hours of hard work may be calculated upon, before anything like Comfort can be obtained under such circumstances; and that the People who should be kept fresh for resisting an Attack, are likely to be worn out by their exertions in preparing for it.

This, however, happily, is by far the worst side of the Picture, for with a moderate share of luck, some little Slope or Broken Ground will offer itself; and some Hedge or Ditch, Bank, Wall, Road or Wood, will be found, either placed exactly as if it were there on purpose to be Defended, or a Plan could readily be arranged for turning it to some account. An Eye is put into a Man's head to be made use of, and it only requires a little previous exercise of that organ, to see all these Natural Intrenchments and local advantages in almost every possible circumstance of Ground and Situation.

64. An endeavour will be made to explain by the Sketches in the annexed Plates, in reference to the Second Class of Works adverted to in No. 26, the simple means which are most in use, and which appear adapted for improving, and deriving advantage from such Local Objects

PLATE. V.

PLATE. VI.

DEFENCE OF HEDGES, ROADS, &c. 29

as are most commonly met with, in the hope of showing, that by the JUDICIOUS APPLICATION OF A VERY LITTLE LABOUR, a serious, and in some cases an almost insurmountable Obstruction, may be formed.

FIG. 17—represents a Hedge on the top of a steep Bank, which has been cut down within 2 feet of the ground: the Branches have been carried to the front as an Obstacle, and two small Steps have been made on the Slope, the one to load on, the other to fire from.

FIG. 18—is supposed to be the same Situation, but Defended in an opposite direction. The Hedge might be felled as an Obstacle, leaving the Stumps 2 feet high to screen the Men, or it might be cut thin and left standing, if it were considered better. The Slope in Front is made steeper, and a little hollow is made to fire from, kneeling.

FIG. 19—A Ditch on the side of the Enemy is supposed to have been deepened, and the Earth and Sods formed into a Breastwork on the reverse of the Hedge; where a small Trench has also been made, to obtain additional Cover.

FIG. 20—The same, fronting the other way; the Hedge felled as an Obstruction, or cut thin, so as to give no Cover to an Enemy, and left standing. The Ditch deepened to 6 feet, and a small Breastwork made from the earth thrown out of it, and from a Trench in the rear.

FIG. 21—A Double Post and Rail. Brushwork is interlaced in the front rail as an Obstacle, and a Breastwork is made leaning against the other, to afford Cover.

FIG. 22—A Bank, with double ditch. One Ditch has been deepened, and the other partly filled up.

FIG. 23—The edge of a Quarry, or steep Bank: a very defensible situation.

DEFENCE OF HEDGES, ROADS, &c.

Fig. 24—A wet Ditch, or Brook. The Breastwork made rom a Trench in the rear.

Fig. 25—A Road. Both Fences felled as Obstructions, and a Breastwork placed for defending them.

Fig. 26—A Hollow Road, arranged in a similar manner.

Figs. 27 & 28—Are Profiles on a bare Steep Rock, to show the way of obtaining Cover in such situations; but where means are so very obvious, it perhaps might not be considered *complimentary* to multiply Examples.

65. It may be remarked, that as Obstructions placed under a close fire in front of Temporary Works are essential to their being properly defended, it will be a consideration whether a Hedge would be more conveniently converted into such an Obstruction as in Fig. 20, or be made to form part of a Breastwork, as in Fig. 18.

A strong growing Hedge is of great value for either purpose : Hunting Men will bear witness that there is many a *big* Fence, across the verdant Fields of Leicestershire, that is not to be got over by Man or Beast, except here and there at some *Soft place,* in single file. And who has ever been out Shooting, and has not now and then fallen in with a puzzler. A small weak Fence, for instance, leaning towards him from the top of a Bank, a thing that looked like nothing, but that took him something like five minutes to get over ; which five minutes, if spent within 15 yards of a posted Enemy, would have afforded time for about twelve rounds being quietly fired into his Body by each Man who could see him.

66. Before setting his Men to Work, it would be necessary that an Officer should have a notion of the Time it would take to execute his projected Defences; for this

PLATE.VII.

purpose he might pace the whole length of his proposed Line, and then by forming an idea how long it would take one Man to finish a certain portion of it, say 4 or 5 yards in length, of deepening a Ditch, scarping a Bank, or felling a Fence, he would see whether the number of men at his disposal could complete the whole in a given time, and would curtail or enlarge his Plan accordingly, and distribute his Men at intervals of 4 or 5, or 7 or 8 yards, as the case might be; for it is impossible to offer any defined Rules which shall apply where circumstances are ever varying. This however must be borne in mind, that there is *more wisdom in doing a little well, than in attempting too much.*

A Stick may be cut for measuring out the portions, and Stakes may be driven in for explaining the Slopes and the general form of the Profile that is required.

Defence of Walls.

67. Walls are readily made available for purposes of Defence by Loop-holing them, the mode of doing it varying with their height and situation.

68. It is a General Rule, that Loop-holes must be so placed, as that an Enemy, if he succeeds in rushing up, shall not be able to reach so as to make use of them; for it is clear, that if he stands on the same level as the Defenders, the Loop-hole would be adapted for serving the convenience of *both* parties, which is not their object.

To obviate this inconvenience, Loop-holes should be placed 8 or 9 feet above the ground on the Outside, but on the Inside, the Banquette, or Step from which the Defenders are to fire, should not be more than about 4 feet 6 inches below them, which may be assumed as a convenient height for the purpose, as already explained in treating of Breastworks. A portion of the wall also, not less than 18 inches high, should be left *above* the Loop-holes, where there is opportunity, for the purpose of securing the Men's Heads when giving their Fire.

69. These points are attainable in several ways, and circumstances must decide which is the most convenient; for example, if a Wall were 10 feet high, the Loop-holes might be pierced within 18 inches of the top, and a Temporary Stage might be made of Casks, Waggons, Ladders, &c., or an earthen Banquette might be thrown up inside for the people to fire from. Fig. 29. And in cases where a very determined Resistance was to be made, a second row of Loop-holes might be arranged, as shown in that Figure. On the other hand, if a wall were only 6 feet high, the Loop-holes might be pierced 4 feet 6 inches above the level on the inside, and a Ditch cut on the outside to obtain the requisite height, which arrangement would save the trouble of making any Banquette. Fig. 30.

70. The quickest way of making a Loop-hole is to break a Wall down from the top to a depth of 2 feet, in the form of a narrow fissure, at intervals of 3 feet or more apart, and as this can be done with common Pickaxes if there are no better Tools at hand, it will generally be found a more convenient mode than cutting them through the Wall, when Time is an object. Such Loop-holes will appear as shown in Fig. 31; it will be seen that they are not quite so safe to fire from as others, but this inconvenience may be partially remedied by filling the upper part with a Stone, a log of Wood, a Sand-bag, &c.

PLATE. VIII.

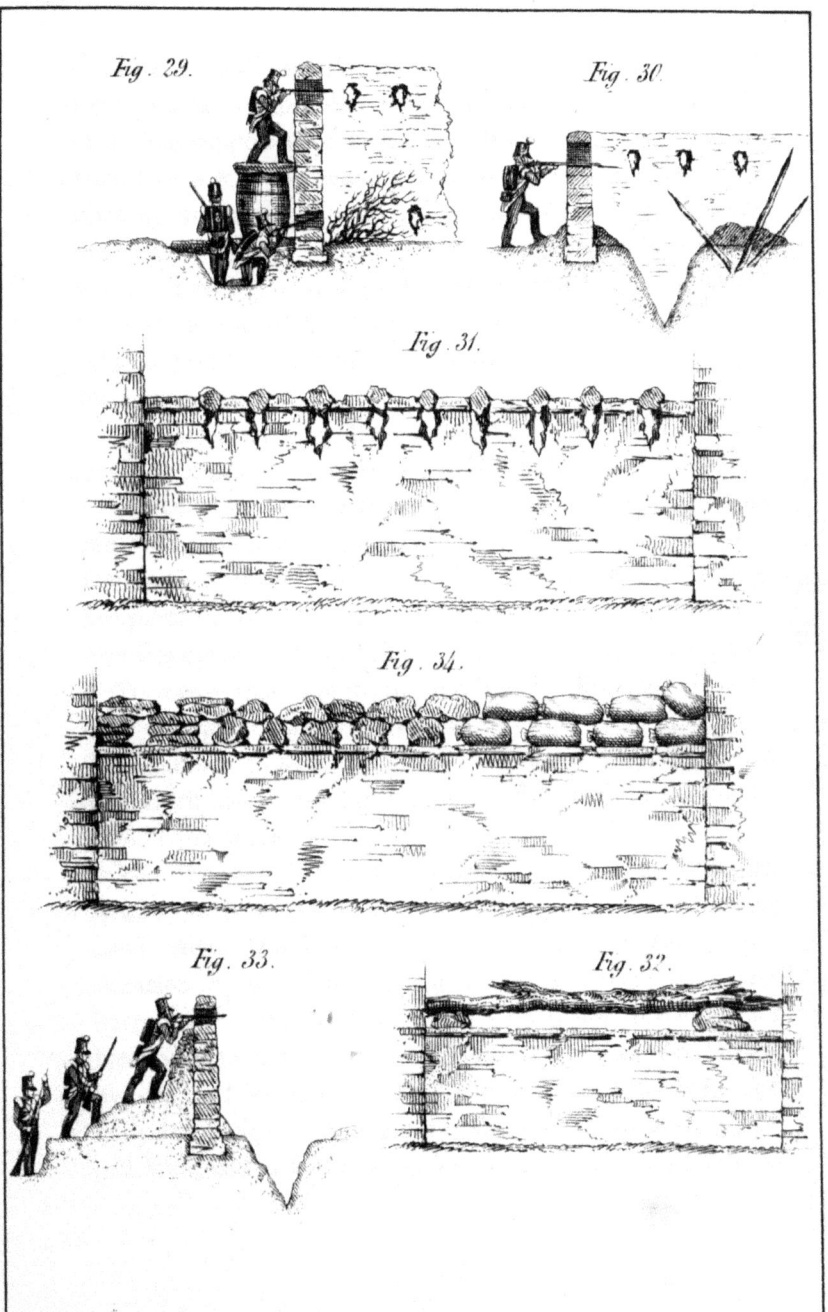

DEFENCE OF WALLS.

71. If a wall should be very low, or there were not time to make Loop-holes, a piece of Timber, or the Trunk of a Tree supported by a couple of Stones, on the top of it, would be a ready expedient, and Men could fire from the opening under it. FIG. 32. Or Sand-bags, if they were at hand, might be laid there, having Loop-holes between them. FIG. 34. Or large Stones or Sods might be placed there in default of Sand-bags. A man of resource would seldom find any difficulty in appropriating something to his purpose.

72. The temporary Loop-holes that are made in Walls or Buildings, are not of course confined to any regular form; they are merely Holes to fire through, made in the required direction, and so as to see the ground from within a few yards of the foot of the Wall or Building in which they are pierced, to the extreme range of a Firelock, affording also the opportunity of firing a little to the right and left.

To secure these points, the absolute Dimensions will vary with the thickness and height of the Wall; the width of the Hole outside, however, need not exceed about 3 inches; but the width inside should, if possible, be equal to the thickness of the Wall.

73. The best Tools for breaking Loop-holes through Brickwork or Masonry, are short Iron Bars, steeled at the head, called Hand-borers. They are held in the proper situation by one Man, and struck with a Sledge-hammer by another. But if People are employed who have not been accustomed to the use of such Tools, they would perhaps get on better each Man with a Crow-bar, which any body can handle. A beginning might be made on the face of a Wall with a Pickaxe, which would very much facilitate

proceedings. The Time it will take to break through a Wall, will be best determined by a Trial on the Spot; for Materials are so very various, it might lead to erroneous conclusions, were any attempt made to state a general Average. Much also would depend on the Tools and Workmen, which adds to the difficulty of offering any precise Data.

74. A Wall exposed to the fire of Artillery, will not afford very pleasant Cover, in consequence of the Splinters that will fly from the Materials whenever it is struck; but if Time admits of it, this inconvenience may in some measure be obviated, by sinking a Trench a few yards in the Rear, and throwing the earth up against the *Inside* of the Wall; or a Ditch may be sunk on the Outside, and the earth be thrown over, as shown in FIG. 33. The Trench is best, as it will give additional protection to the Men; but the Ditch may be required as an obstacle, or to give height to the Loop-holes, and therefore as usual, circumstances must decide what is best to be done. It is not contemplated that there would be opportunity for giving this embankment sufficient thickness to make it Shot-proof, but most of the Splinters would bury themselves, if it were only 3 or 4 feet thick, and "*Half a loaf is better than no bread.*"

STOCKADE WORK.

75. Stockade Work may be substituted with advantage for Breastworks, when there is Timber to be had in abundance, especially if it can be Covered from the Fire of Artillery. It has this advantage over Earthen Works of

PLATE.IX.

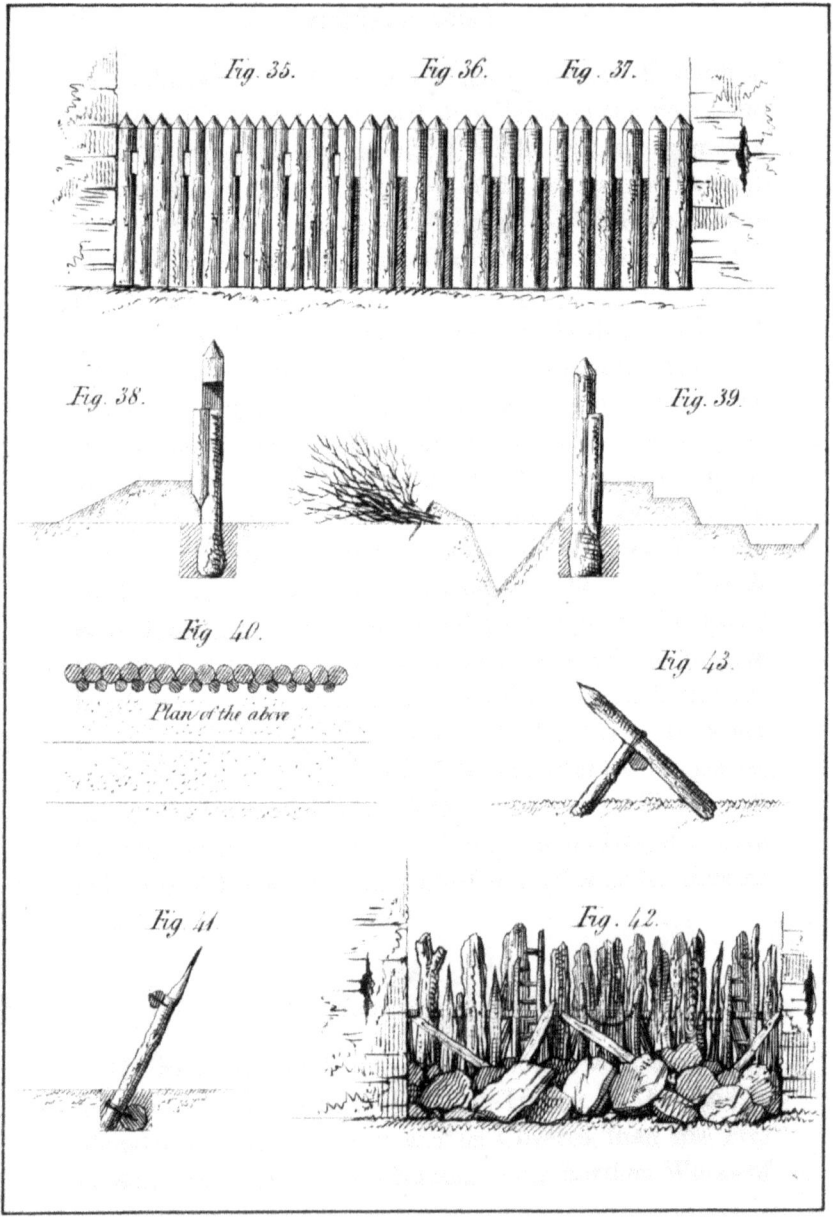

STOCKADE WORK.

very small Profile, that if made high enough, it is not easily got over, and therefore in itself it opposes an Obstacle to an Enemy, which they generally do not.

Stockade Work may be made with the rough Trunks of young Trees, cut into lengths of 12 or 14 feet, and averaging not less than from 10 to 15 inches in diameter. They should be firmly planted, upright, in a narrow Ditch, 3 or 4 feet deep, either close together, or with intervals of a few inches for Firing through. The interstices in either case should be filled up to a certain distance, with shorter pieces of Timber, to protect the Men, as will be better understood by referring to Figs. 39 and 40; and the Loop-holes should be arranged with the precautions adverted to in No. 68.

A Banquette or Step will generally be required on the Inside; and a Ditch, and any other Obstacle on the Outside, that can be made in the Time, will add to the difficulties of an Assault. See Fig. 39. In defending a Stockade, the means of stopping up any partial Breaches which may be made by Artillery, should be at hand, and a Flank Fire across the Front is very essential, as it will be obvious that were an Enemy to succeed in rushing up to it, he would be under Cover from the direct Fire of the Loop-holes.

Chap. V.—Obstructions.

76. Obstructions in front of Temporary Works of inconsiderable Profile, are essential to their being vigorously Defended, and various expedients have been devised, some of which it will be well to explain.

An Abattis is perhaps the best Obstruction that can be formed in a limited time. It is made by felling a number of Trees, if they are on the spot, and laying them side by side, with the branches towards an Enemy, and interlaced as much as possible. Small twigs should be cut off, and the projecting points sharpened. If the Trees are so large that they cannot easily be displaced, no precaution is necessary for securing them; but if they are smaller, they must be confined in their places by driving Stakes among them, and laying heavy Timber on their butt ends, or burying those ends in a small Ditch. If Trees and Brushwood stand pretty thick on the ground, there will be no necessity for placing them in any regular form when cut down, for it has been found on Service, that if permitted to lie as they fall, a most formidable Obstacle will be presented.

For instance, if a Wood or Copse forms part of a Line, a breadth of 20 or 30 yards of it being felled in front of the situation proposed to be taken up for the Defence, would so encumber the ground, that but little else in the way of an Obstruction would be required. A Breastwork behind such an Abattis would give the means of Defence, and if opportunity offered, and the Wood were extensive,

OBSTRUCTIONS. 37

several such Lines might be made and disputed in succession.*

In wooded countries these Breastworks may be made of Trunks of Trees, cut into lengths, and piled one upon the other, to the required height, which affords a means of obtaining Cover very quickly, if there are a few Workmen who understand laying about them with an Axe.

Stumps should be left of different heights, varying with their size; those that are large enough to conceal a man, should be cut as near as may be to the ground, but it will be useful to leave smaller ones, some 4 or 5 feet high. If these latter, instead of being entirely separated, are only half cut through, and the heads pulled down, and interlaced among the other stumps, in the way in which a growing hedge is "pleached," it would puzzle the Devil himself to get through such an Entanglement under a close Fire, provided there were enough Trees on the spot to make it perfect. There used to be a blackthorn Cover, of only a few acres in extent, overlooking the Vale of Belvoir, and not 100 miles from Melton, which had been laid down as an Abattis of this sort, for the better protection and security of that valued animal, the Fox; and many is the time, when *Mr. Pug* has kept close, that it has taken the best pack of hounds in England 20 minutes to go through it, though each particular dog was as *au fait* as a Hedgehog in working his way among thorns. A Grenadier would have had no chance at all.

---

* It was from a strong Abattis of this description that Colonel De Salaberry, with a handful of Canadian Voltigeurs, successfully disputed the advance of an American Army on the line of the Chateaugay River, in 1813, during the late War in Canada.

77. PALISADES form a very good Obstruction, especially if protected from the effects of Artillery; and if the means are at hand, they are soon planted.

An expeditious mode of doing it, is to sink a small Ditch, about 2 feet 6 inches deep, and the same breadth, and to nail the ends of the Palisades to a piece of Timber, or the Trunk of a Tree laid on the bottom of it, and then fill in the earth, and ram it well. FIG. 41.

The Palisades should be 9 or 10 feet long, so that when finished, the ends shall be at least 7 feet above the ground. They may be made out of the stems of young Trees of 6 or 8 inches diameter; but stout Rails, Gates with the ends knocked off, Planks split in half, Cart shafts, Ladders, and a variety of such things, will come into play, where more regular Palisades are not to be had. If the Materials are weak, a cross piece must be nailed to them near the top, to prevent their being broken down, and they must not be placed so close together as to cover an Enemy. FIG. 42.

78. CHEVAUX DE FRISE of a temporary nature may be made for stopping up an outlet through a Barricade, or for adding to the defence of a Door-way, or cutting off the Communication between different parts of a Post, &c. It will differ little from Palisades as to Scantling, &c., and its general form and proportion will be understood on referring to FIG. 43. The ends of the Stakes should stand from 5 to 7 feet above the ground, and be strong enough to resist any attempt to break them, and there should be as many short legs, as long Stakes, otherwise a few handy fellows, with Axes, might let it down. If it is to be removed for the convenience of passing, it should be made in lengths

proportionate to the weight; and when so arranged, the means should be at hand for chaining or otherwise securing the lengths together.

79. A good Obstruction might be made out of common sheep Hurdles, planted in rows, at 8 or 10 feet distance, and leaning a little to the front, in which direction they are very awkward to get over. Stiff Brushwood interlaced would add to their effect; or Stakes driven firmly into the ground, and plenty of them, are not easily passed over in close order.

80. Holes about 3 feet deep and the same diameter, usually called Trap Holes, dug in rows as if for planting trees, and the earth out of them piled up in small heaps, would materially interfere with regular and rapid movement, and if Time admitted, the depth might be increased so as to present a more formidable Obstruction.

81. Many other Temporary expedients would naturally suggest themselves under the difference of circumstances that are to be met with at every step. It should ever be remembered that whatever will cramp and impede the steady movement of a Column, and detain it under a close Fire for however short a period, is *worth having*, and should not be neglected. Where a mighty Abattis could not be formed, perhaps a Cabbage Garden could be found, and even that would be *better than nothing*, inasmuch as it would be preferable to a Bowling Green, over which people could come at a racing pace to the Assault of a small Work.

82. As it is wisdom on all occasions to give an Enemy full credit for doing his utmost, it would be well not to be deceived by appearances, but to subject an Abattis or any other Obstruction to a Trial, before coming to any conclu-

sion as to its efficiency; for if one Man could get over or through it, with his Arms and Accoutrements on, another could do the same. Some people have a way of allowing their wishes and hopes to deceive their judgment, which does not signify much if the effect only falls on themselves, but is of importance to be guarded against, in cases where others are included among the sufferers, if a mistake be made.

83. It would have been desirable to have conveyed an idea of the Time in which a certain length of Stockade or Palisading could be executed, but this kind of work is influenced by so many circumstances, such as the Quantity, Size, and Nature of the Materials, the Expertness of the Workmen, &c., that were any Data offered, it would be more likely to embarrass, and lead to erroneous conclusions, than to be of any assistance in enabling an Officer to form an accurate opinion when applying them.

If, however, he determined to make the attempt to construct something of the kind, he could never go wrong in setting the greater proportion of his Men to work, in the first instance, in collecting an abundance of Materials, and depositing them in convenient situations for being afterwards worked up.

To prevent confusion, it would be well to divide his Men into small Squads, of eight or ten each, for this duty; and to prescribe to each where they were to obtain Materials, and of what description, whether by felling Trees in the neighbourhood, unroofing Houses, taking up Floors, &c., and where each Squad was to deposit what it procured.

When the quantity began to accumulate, all the Carpenters might be employed in preparing the *Stuff*, whilst

OBSTRUCTIONS. 41

some Labourers working in Line, at 6 feet apart, were sinking the Ditch, into which the Pickets were to be planted, No. 79; and when this was deep enough, a proportion of the Carpenters, assisted by Labourers, might commence fixing them.

If Time were an object, which is supposed throughout these pages, and there were plenty of hands, the business of fixing the Stockade or Palisading should be undertaken iu distinct portions, that there might be no confusion in employing as many Men as could work to advantage at the same time. For instance, one Carpenter and two Labourers might be told off to every 10 or 12 feet, and with exertion and good arrangement, a very respectable appearance ought to be made in a few hours, under ordinary circumstances.

Chap. VI.—Of Placing Buildings, &c. in a state of Defence.

84. If a Building forms part of a general Line of Defence, or is in the Contour of the Works round a Town or Village, the front and sides only may require being prepared for Defence, for a Force must not be shut up without a special object; if, on the contrary, it is an Independent Post, to be defended to the last, and is open to attack on all sides, every point must be equally looked to, and the means of retreat and of re-enforcing it, must be preserved, if considered necessary under the circumstances.

85. The great art of making a Defensible Post out of Buildings, and the Outhouses and Walls that usually surround them, consists in selecting from the mass of Objects before you what will answer the purpose, and sacrificing everything else, making use of the Materials to strengthen the part you wish to fortify. It is more difficult to state any precise Rules for such proceedings, than for laying out Works in the Field, for in one case you generally have a choice in the form of your intended Works, and a better opportunity of arranging what you have to execute under the direction of some General Principles, but in the other you must take what you find, and all you have to do, is to *make the best of it.*

86. The Principles of Defence adverted to in Nos. 12 to 23, must be taken into consideration as far as they will apply, and if with a knowledge of these Principles an Officer is practically acquainted with the Means that are

usually employed for strengthening such Posts, a very little experience will enable him to arrange his Plan, and set his Men to work with a confident expectation, that in a very few hours he will be able to enliven a peaceable domicile, by converting it into a respectable Fortress.

87. The Objects now under consideration are Churches, Country-houses, Factories, Prisons, or other substantial Buildings; and as there is but little difference in the mode to be pursued for placing any of them in a state of Defence, an explanation of the details applied to a single House, will perhaps be sufficient to convey an idea on the subject.

88. What has been before said in Nos. 26 to 42, of the points requiring attention in the selection of a Military Post, will be applicable if a choice is to be made among Buildings; thus, a Building proper for defensive purposes, should possess some or all of the following requisites :—

First. It should COMMAND all that surrounds it.

Second. Should be SUBSTANTIAL, and of a Nature to furnish Materials useful for placing it in a state of Defence.

Third. Should be of an EXTENT PROPORTIONED TO THE NUMBER OF DEFENDERS, and only require the TIME AND MEANS which can be devoted to completing it.

Fourth. Should have Walls and Projectings that mutually FLANK each other.

Fifth. Should be DIFFICULT OF ACCESS on the side exposed to Attack, and yet have a SAFE RETREAT for the Defenders.

Sixth. And be in a Situation proper for fulfilling the Object for which the Detachment is to be posted.

A Church will be found more usually to unite all these good properties than any other Building.

89. It may be remarked that though good strong Walls are an advantage, yet their Thickness should be limited to 2 or 3 feet, from the difficulty there would be in piercing Loop-holes; unless when they are likely to be battered by Artillery, in which case the Musketry must be confined to the Windows, and the more solid the Walls are, the better. It should also be remembered that Brick Houses and Walls are preferable, on several accounts, to those built of Stone; for when exposed to Artillery, a Round Shot merely makes a small hole in the former, but Stone is broken up in large masses, and dangerous Splinters fly from it in all directions. It is much easier also to make Loop-holes through Brick-work than through Masonry. Wooden Houses, or those made of Plaster, are to be avoided, from the facility with which an Enemy can set Fire to them, and they are frequently not even Musket-proof. Thatched houses are equally objectionable, on account of fire, unless there is time to unroof them; and after all it must not be forgotten, that earthen works when exposed to Artillery, are to be preferred to houses, as far as affording security to the defenders is concerned. In seeking this security, however, it should be borne in mind that they are not so *Defensible;* for Troops cannot be run into in a House, but they are not exempt from such an intrusion in an Earthen Work of the nature under discussion. The two together can be made to form a more respectable Post than *either* can be made into singly, for the merits of both will be enhanced, and the defects be modified, by the union. A Building is therefore at all times a capital base to go to work upon.

IN A STATE OF DEFENCE.   45

The Walls may be partially protected from Cannon Shot by throwing up Earthen Parapets round it, and the House may " reciprocate" by acting the part of a Keep, and afford the Garrison a place of refuge, in which they may either defend themselves with advantage, or if it "suits their book," resume the offensive and drive the assailants out again.

90. An Officer will be able to make his selection at first sight, with reference to most of these points, but it requires a little more consideration to determine whether a Building and its appliances are convertible into a Post, of a Size proportioned to the Force under his command. The average number of Men, however, proper for the defence of a House, may be roughly estimated on some such Data as the following :—That in a Lower story it might generally be proper to tell off one Man for every 4 feet that the Walls measured round the Interior.* In the Second Story One Man for every 6 Feet, and in an Attic or Roof One Man for every 8 Feet. For example, if a House of three Stories high were found on pacing it to measure 140 feet round the interior Walls, the number of men for its defence on the above Data would be determined thus:—

Feet.

$\frac{140}{4}$ Would give 35; which would be the number of Men for the Lower Story.

$\frac{140}{6}$ Would be about 23 Men for the Second Floor.

$\frac{140}{8}$ Would be 18 Men for the Attic.

---

* Pacing round the outside of the House, and making an allowance for the thickness of the Walls, would be the easiest way of determining the interior dimensions.

making a total of 76 Men for the three Stories; to which about one-sixth of the whole, say 14 men, should be added as a Reserve, making altogether a Garrison of 90 men. If there were Out-buildings or Walls in addition, the number of Men required for their Defence, would be determined in a similar manner, by assuming certain Data adapted to the circumstances as a guide in the calculation.

91. These numbers are not to be considered *definitive*, but merely to convey an idea on the subject; for if a Detachment were much weaker in proportion to the Extent, a vigorous defence might still be made. The Force might be concentrated where most required, as it is not a matter of course that a place will be attacked on all sides at once; or if a Building were found so large that the disposable Force would be too much disseminated, or if there were a want of Materials and Time for putting the *whole* of it in a State of Defence, a *part* of it only might be occupied.

92. Should there exist any doubt about having sufficient Time to complete all that might be wished, it would become matter for consideration what were the Points which it would be of the greatest importance to secure First, so as to be in a condition to repel an *immediate* Attack, because such Points would naturally claim attention to the exclusion of all others.

In such a case, it might be well to employ as many men as could work without hindering each other by being too crowded.

First. To collect Materials and Barricade the Doors and Windows on the Ground Floor, to make Loop-holes in them, and level any Obstruction outside that would give Cover to the Enemy, or materially facilitate the Attack.

Second. To sink Ditches opposite the Doors on the outside, and arrange Loop-holes in the Windows of the Upper Story.

Third. To make Loop-holes through the Walls generally, attending first to the most exposed parts, and to break Communications through all the Party Walls and Partitions.

Fourth. To place Abattis or any feasible Obstructions on the Outside, and to improve the Defence of the Post by the construction of Tambours, &c.

Fifth. To place Out-buildings and Garden Walls in a state of Defence, and establish Communications between them. To make arrangements in the Lower Story especially, for defending one Room or Portion after another, so that partial possession only could be obtained on a sudden rush being made. These different Works to be undertaken *in the order of their relative importance,* according to circumstances; and after securing the immediate object for which they were designed, they might remain to be improved upon if opportunity offered.

93. An endeavour will now be made to explain the mode of executing these Works in the order in which they are mentioned.

Collecting Materials.

The Materials that will be found most useful in Barricading the Passages, Doors, and Windows, are Boxes, Casks, Cart Bodies, Bricks, Stones, Cinders, Dung, &c.,

and Timber of any sort that comes to hand, which, if it cannot be found elsewhere on the Premises, the Roof and Floors must be stripped to furnish what is required.

Barricading Doors.

94. In the application of these Materials, the Boxes and Casks filled with Cinders or Dung, and placed against the Doors to a height of 6 feet, will prevent their being forced open, and Loop-holes may be made through the upper portions, which can be rendered Musket-proof to protect the Men's heads; short lengths of Timber piled one upon another to the same height, leaving a space between any two of them in a convenient situation for Firing through, and their ends being secured in the side walls of a Passage, or propped with upright pieces on the inside, will effect the same object; or a Door may be loosely bricked up, leaving Loop-holes, &c.

If it is probable that Artillery will be brought up for knocking away these Barricades, and so forcing an entrance, a Passage may be partially filled with Dung or Rubbish to the thickness of 8 or 10 feet, or thick Beams of Timber may be reared up on the outside of a Door, and the interval filled with the same, or with earth if more convenient.

A hole, about 3 feet square, may be left through an ordinary Barricade for keeping up a Communication with the Exterior; but for effecting a Retreat, or making Sorties, it will be necessary to make a Door Musket-proof, by nailing on several additional thicknesses of Plank, and arrange it so to open as usual, or to contrive something

PLATE. X.

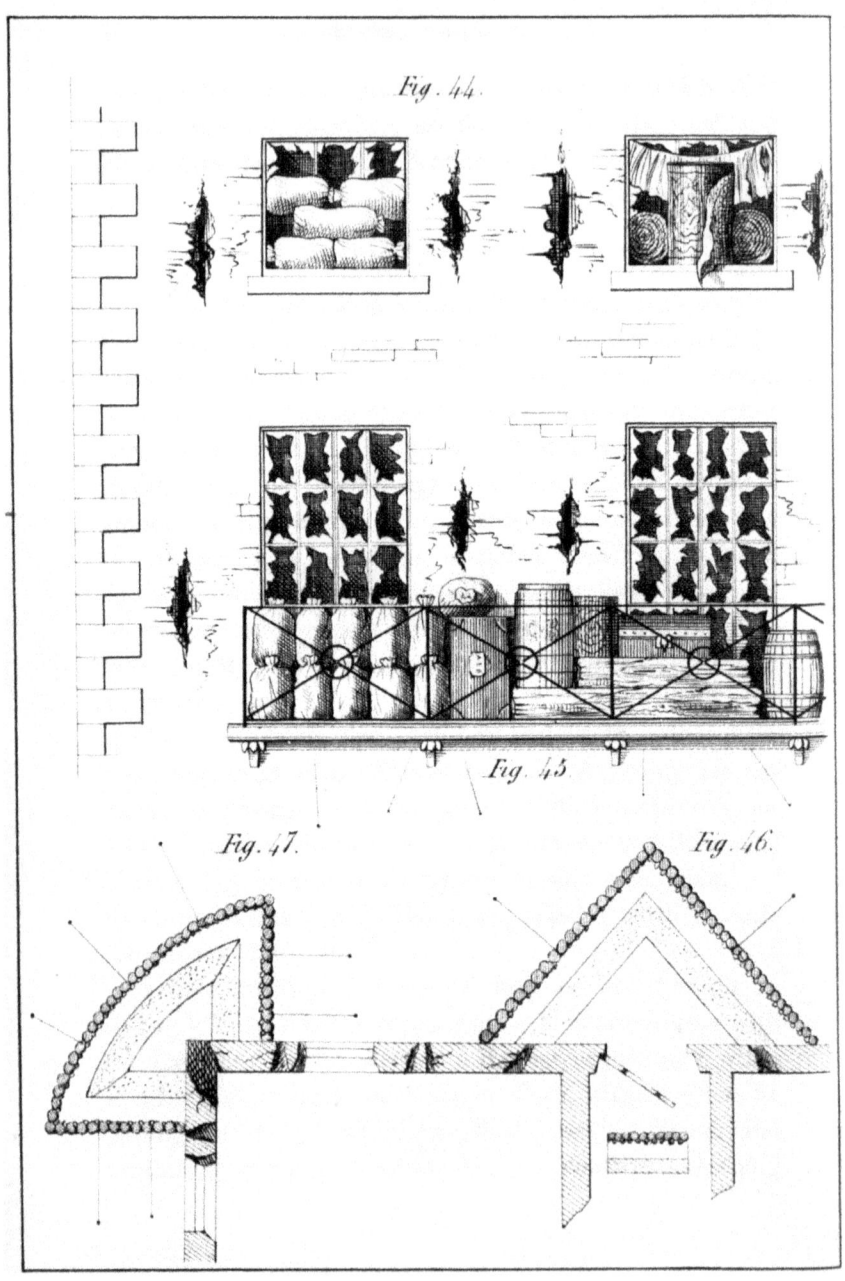

on the spot which shall equally protect the Men when Firing through the Loop-holes, and yet be removable at pleasure.

BARRICADING WINDOWS.

95. Windows do not require to be Barricaded so Strongly as Doors, unless from their Situation an Entrance may easily be effected, or an Escalade be attempted. The principal object is to Screen and Protect the Defenders whilst giving their Fire; anything, therefore, that will fill up the Window to a height of 6 feet from the Floor, and that is Musket-proof, will answer the purpose. Thus two or three rows of filled Sand-bags, laid in the sill of a Window, FIG. 44, or short lengths of Timber would do; or a Carpet, a Mattrass, or Blankets rolled up, would be ready Expedients. Loop-holes would in all cases be arranged whatever Materials were used. If Time presses, and Windows could not be blocked up, one means of obtaining concealment, which is the next best thing to security, would be to hang a great Coat or Blanket across the lower part of them as a Screen, and make the Men fire beneath it, kneeling on the Floor. The Glass should be removed from Windows before an Attack commences, as it is liable to injure the Defenders, when broken by Musketry.

LEVELLING OBSTRUCTIONS OUTSIDE.

96. Any Shrubberies, Fences, or Out-Buildings, within Musket-shot, which would favour an attack by affording Cover to an Enemy, and allowing him to approach unper-

ceived, should be got rid of as soon as possible. The Trees should be felled, leaving the Stumps of different heights, so as to encumber the ground, and the Materials of Walls, &c. should be spread about with the same view; but whatever is convertible for Barricades should be carried to the house. The Thatch from Roofs, and any Combustibles, should also be removed or destroyed.

Ditches in front of the Doors, &c.

97. As a means of preventing a Door being forced, a Ditch may be dug in front of it, about 7 feet wide and 5 feet deep; such a Ditch is also necessary in front of the Lower Windows, if the Loop-holes cannot be conveniently made high enough from the Outside to prevent an Enemy reaching them, for the reasons before explained in the Defence of Walls. No. 68. These partial Ditches may afterwards be converted into a continued Ditch all round a House if opportunity offers, as it would contribute to the Defence of the Post. The Floors may also be taken up on the inside, opposite the Doors or Windows open to attack.

Loop-holes.

98. If the Walls are not too thick, they may be pierced for Loop-holes, at every 3 feet, in the spaces between the Windows, &c. Fig. 44. The dimensions, and mode of executing these Loop-holes, has been already described in treating of the Defence of Walls, Nos. 68 and 72, and in the Figures to which they refer.

Two Tier of these Loop-holes may be made if opportunity offers, and a temporary Scaffolding of Furniture, Benches, Casks, or Ladders, &c. erected for Firing from the upper ones: on the Lower story a row of Loop-holes may be made close to the ground. The Floor must, in this case, be partly removed, and a small Excavation made between the beams for the convenience of making use of them. Just under the Eaves of a Roof there is generally a place where Loop-holes can be made with great facility, and a Tile or Slate knocked out here and there with a Musket, will give other openings, from which an Assailant may be well plied as he comes up.

Communications.

99. A clear Communication must be made round the Whole Interior of the Building, by breaking through all Partitions that interfere with it: and for the same purpose, if Houses stand in a Row or Street, the Party Walls must be opened, so as to have free Access from one end to the other. Means should likewise be at hand for Closing these Openings against an Enemy, who may have obtained any partial possession. Holes may also be made in the Upper Floors to Fire on the Assailants, if they force the Lower ones, and arrangements made for blocking up the Staircases, with some such expedient as a Tree, prepared in the same manner as for an Abattis, or by having a rough Pallisade Gate placed across. Balconies may be covered or filled up in front with Timber or Sand-bags, and made use of to Fire from downwards. Fig. 45.

ABATTIS.

100. The partial levelling of any object on the Outside, that would give Concealment to an Enemy, and favour an Attack, is supposed to have been already attended to: but if Time admits, after the Loop-holes, &c. are completed; this system must be extended and perfected, and the formation of a more regular Abattis should be commenced, and any other Obstruction added that opportunity permits. The best Distance for such Obstructions, if they are continuous and cannot be turned, is within 20 or 30 yards of a Work, or even less, so that every shot may tell whilst the Assailants are detained in forcing a passage through them; within such a distance also of Defenders securely posted, it would not be pleasant for a Hostile Force in confusion, to "*Fall in,*" or "*Re-form Column.*" No. 21. If Hand-Grenades are to play their part in the Defence of a Post, the Obstruction, whatever it may be, should be placed within their influence. A man will easily throw them 20 yards, but a trial on the spot will best determine the distance at which they can be used with effect.

TAMBOURS.

101. If the Building that has been selected has no Porches, Wings, or Projecting Portions from which Flank Defence can be obtained, it will be advisable to construct something of a temporary nature to afford it.

Stockade Work offers a ready means of effecting this object; it may be disposed in the form of a triangle, projecting 8 or 10 feet in front of a door or window, Fig.

46, planted in the manner, and with the precautions of having the Loop-holes high enough, as described in No. 68. A small hole should be left in the Barricade of the door or window to communicate with the interior. Three or four Loop-holes on each face of the projection, cut between the timbers, will be found very useful in the Defence. These contrivances are usually termed Tambours, and if constructed at the angle of a Building, will Flank two sides of it. FIG. 47.

OUT-BUILDINGS AND WALLS.

102. When the defences of the Main Building are in a state of forwardness, any Out-buildings or Walls which have been found too solid to be levelled at the moment, or which have been preserved for the chance of having Time to fortify them, and thus to increase the strength of the Post, must be looked to. They may be placed in a state of defence by the means already described, and separate communications should be established between them and the principal Building by a Trench, or a Line of Stockade work, and by breaking through the Walls when necessary. In this way a Post may be enlarged in any required proportion, by turning all objects that present themselves, such as Out-buildings, Sheds, Walls, Hedges, Ponds, &c. to the best account; first taking the precaution to secure what is absolutely necessary for *immediate* protection, and for placing it in a state to be defended on the shortest notice.

103. An Exterior Wall or Fence, tolerably close to a House and parallel to it, may be retained for the purposes

of Defence, without the danger of affording Cover, and thus facilitating an Attack, by throwing up a Slope of earth on the outside of it, or planting an abattis in the same situation. Fig. 48. An Enemy would thus remain completely exposed, and it would be worse than useless to him.

104. If a Post of the description under consideration were composed of two or more Buildings, and it were to be left to itself, and were open to attack on all sides, the Stockades or Trenches, forming the Communications between them, would obviously require to be so arranged as to afford Cover, and the Means of Resistance *on both sides*. This would be effected by merely making them *double*, as shown in Figs. 49 and 50; but for greater security, the exterior of such Communications should be laid under Fire from the Buildings at their extremities. If Cover cannot from circumstances be obtained, Screens should be contrived that will conceal the movements that may be necessary.

105. In arranging the defences of such Posts, it is an essential point to make each portion of them so far independent of the others, that if any one part, such as a Building for instance, be taken, it shall not compromise the safety of the remainder, nor materially impair the defence they will make by themselves; so that whilst free Communications are essential in most cases to a vigorous defence, the means must be at hand for instantly cutting them off by some such expedients as would be afforded, by a Loopholed Musket-proof Door, or rough Gates, or by letting fall a Tree, prepared as for an Abattis, and which till wanted might be reared on its end in the situation required;

PLATE XI.

PLATE XII.

Fig. 51.

PLATE XIII.

Fig. 52.

having previously secured the means of bringing a close fire upon it.

106. It is incredible what a Defence may be made in a substantial Building, if it has been properly prepared, and the right sort of people have been put into it. The Siege of Saragossa in 1809, affords a proof of how much may be done in defending Streets and Houses. The French were reduced to the delay of an attack, *secundem artem*, and no impression was made but by the regular means of Artillery and Mines. It is to be recollected, however, that the Houses could not be set on fire, and the Walls were of extraordinary thickness.

Figs. 51 and 52, are given as examples of a Country-house and Out-buildings which have been prepared for defence in the manner described, at a considerable sacrifice of the picturesque; but with that we have nothing to do.

Chap. VII.—Defence of Villages.

107. Though placing a Village in a state of defence argues that larger Forces, and Officers of higher rank and more experience are engaged, than has hitherto been contemplated in the smaller Posts that have been discussed in this little Treatise; yet, in cases of emergency, much responsibility may still devolve on a young Officer in executing, and in some measure planning portions of the work; the subject therefore will be briefly noticed, though the details already entered into, embrace much of the information which would enable him to make himself useful on such an occasion.

108. As a Village is only the extension of a smaller Post of the same nature, the general requisites adverted to in Nos. from 26 to 42, in treating of such Posts, should be looked for, in determining whether or no it is favorable for Defensive purposes, and whether it offers such facilities for executing the necessary Works, as that they can be completed in the Time that can be devoted to them.

Thus a Village should not be commanded;—it should furnish Materials proper for its defence, and be of a nature not easily set on fire;—of a size proportioned to the Force designed to occupy it;—should be difficult of access, &c. In addition to which there should be some Substantial Buildings near the Exterior, to be converted into strong salient points of the general line. And in most cases a Church or large building in the Interior, to serve as a Keep, would be a desideratum. There should likewise be a facility for forming a connected line all round, or on the front and flanks, if they only were to be fortified. If it were situated on a height, some of the sides of which were inaccessible, or if it were partially skirted by a River or Marsh, so much the better; it would be more easily rendered defensible.

109. An idea may be formed of the Extent the Works should have in reference to the disposable Force, by making a rough estimate on the principles advanced in Nos. 38 and 92, bearing in mind that they will admit of considerable latitude either way.

110. Villages may be required to be Intrenched under a variety of circumstances, but as far as the Works themselves are concerned, two cases only require consideration, *viz.*, when they are left *Open in the Rear*, and when they are *Enclosed all round*.

111. Under the first consideration;—If a Village is to be held as an Advanced Post, or forms part of a general line, in front of an Army, and that it can receive instant Support when attacked, it will generally be left *Open in the Rear*, and only be strengthened in Front. To effect this, the first attention of an Officer, after determining his General Plan on the Principles already laid down, would be directed to the readiest means of stopping up all the Streets, Roads, and Lanes on the Front and Flanks of the exposed side, with such temporary Obstructions as could be most expeditiously formed.

Men would be detached to bring to the spot selected, whatever Materials would assist in the work, such as Waggons, Carts, Ploughs, Harrows, Trees, Gates, rows of Paling, Furniture, Chains, Ropes, &c. With these there would be no difficulty in creating Obstructions in a very little time, that would interfere with the visits of Cavalry, or break the order of Infantry, and thus offer impediments to an immediate Attack. They should be placed in those situations where they would afterwards be of some use, either as Obstacles in front of other Works proposed to be executed, or in the principal line itself, and therefore to be improved upon; for if possible NO LABOUR SHOULD BE THROWN AWAY.

112. Whilst these Works were in progress, an Officer would have more leisure to examine his whole Post in detail, in doing which he would find it convenient to make a memorandum of the number of men that could be employed to advantage, and the probable time it would require to complete each of the Works he proposes for its Defence, so as to suit them to his means. No. 48. These being afterwards confided in distinct portions to the active superintendence of intelligent young Officers, would ensure their being done in less time than were he to attempt *ubiquity*, in looking after them all himself.

113. In arranging his General Plan, he will have selected, as far as circumstances have favoured him, some good substantial Buildings, not exceeding the effective range of a musket, say 150 or 200 yards apart, for the most prominent or salient points of his line, which will be prepared for Defence, as explained in the foregoing pages; or he will have decided on occupying those points with the best Breastworks or Stockades he can make in the time, Nos. 57 and 75; and availing himself of all Buildings, Hedges, Ditches, Walls, or Inequalities that lie between them, he would proceed to make arrangements for con-

necting them by Breastworks, Trenches, Stockades, or some other of the means already described, and on the principles laid down respecting Flank defence, and giving a good Fire to the front. His Working Parties would be distributed accordingly, and it would be his constant endeavour to obtain the best Cover, and to create the greatest Obstructions, with the least possible labour. No exertion should be spared until the enclosure were perfect, and in a state to be defended; all hands should be employed night and day, if necessary, in alternate reliefs, and every arrangement should be made with this view; such points as required the greatest attention might then be progressively improved upon.

114. All the Streets and Roads open to Attack, should be shut up by good Barricades constructed in rear of the temporary Obstructions that have been created. These Barricades may be made, if Time admits, by sinking a Ditch 7 or 8 feet deep, and forming the earth into a substantial Breastwork, Fig. 9, planting Palisades, &c., if opportunity offers. Or if not exposed to Artillery fire, Stockade Work, No. 75, would be very effective; but if Time presses, Casks, Boxes, or Cart bodies, arranged in order and filled with earth, stones, dung, or cinders, would be a ready expedient. Bales of goods, hogsheads of sugar, sacks of corn, or even the rolls of cloth out of a tailor's shop, would be very convertible to *Warlike purposes*, if they came to hand.

The Mass should be raised 6 or 7 feet high, and a Banquette or Step be arranged for Firing over it. No. 3. The access should be as much obstructed as possible, and above all, every House in the neighbourhood should be Loop-holed, so as to give a good Flanking Fire over the ground in their front. FIGS. 14 and 15 may be referred to as examples.

115. If several Barricades, to be disputed in succession, are made in a street, the means of retreat through them must be preserved. This may be effected by disposing the lines as already explained, (FIGS. 11, 12, and 13,) by which the passages would be readily closed and defended; and a communication should be made from house to house on each side the street, for firing on an advancing Column. No. 99.

116. In Front of his Post, it would be an object to destroy all houses within range of Musketry,—to level all Fences, and fill up all Ditches, &c. that ran *parallel* to the general line he had taken up within that distance, so that an enemy might find no cover whatever; such Fences and Obstructions however, as ran *perpendicular* to his Post, and that could be seen from it on both sides, might remain, as they would interfere with the flank movements of an attacking force, and embarrass his approach. Within the line of works, on the contrary, all Fences and Obstructions that are *perpendicular* to the line, and interfere with a free communication from right to left, should be cut away. Those that are *parallel* should be preserved, as affording protection to a retreat and further means of defence, if the outer line were forced. It is very important to have a second or even a third line of defence prepared, if the position of the buildings and localities admit of such an arrangement, so that if Troops are driven from one line by a superior force, they may find another and yet another in their rear, all ready for occupation. If there be any truth

in the proposition we started with, that the object of defensive Works is to enable a small force to cope with a larger one, the defenders ought to have the advantage from first to last, and they should profit by it, as long as ammunition lasts and bayonets can be made use of.

117. Such Posts as these, when situated in a plain before the front of an Army, or as a point of *appui* for one of its wings, have a very important part to play, as was illustrated at Waterloo. But to enable an inferior force to derive the greatest possible advantage from them, they should not only be strengthened in themselves, but every obstruction in rear of them should be levelled, so that there may be facility for the movement of all arms for their immediate support when attacked. If there are fences or walls in existence, which cannot be cleared away, good broad roads should be made through them; on the other hand, if a Force in connexion with such a Post, is on equal terms with an enemy, so that the offensive may be taken up, and a forward movement made, as opportunity offers, it would be injudicious to have Obstructions in front, which might in that case be in the way. It is the old story again, probabilities and circumstances alone can decide what is best to be done; but this only tends to show, that if an officer is to *do his duty* under such circumstances, he must do more than learn the Regulations by heart.

118. Under the second consideration, if a Village were to be occupied as an independent Post, to be defended to the last, energy and intelligence must be drawn upon to the utmost, to place it in the best possible state. The details of execution will be similar to those already explained, as well as the general principles which regulate the whole;

but it must be *enclosed all round* with an outer line, and if possible some strong building, such as a Church or Jail, must be looked up and put in a state of defence, and supplied with provisions, ammunition, &c., to which, as a Citadel or keep, the defenders may retire, if driven in by an overwhelming force, and there fight the battle over again, with a better chance of success.

119. This keep should be centrally situated, in a position covered from the Enemy's Artillery, and commanding the principal roads or streets. It should be of a nature not easily set on fire, and should have good and assured communications with all the out-works. Advantage must be taken of any Walls or Out-buildings surrounding whatever has been selected as a Keep; and they should be converted into out-works, for strengthening it as an independent Post. These out-works are the more necessary, as besides the additional strength they will impart, they will be found of essential service in securing a retreat into it; for a Reserve quietly occupying them, ought to command considerable respect from an enemy, however hotly he might be in pursuit.

If suitable buildings were to be found, and there were men enough to defend them, several such Keeps might be prepared; and on the contrary, if a Village should be of too great an extent for the force thrown into it, a portion of it only might be strengthened, and the remainder be separated or destroyed; or the defence might be confined to some principal building, FIG. 53, taken from sketches inserted in some Instructions published by the French Imperial Minister of War in 1814, and translated by Major (now Lieut.-Colonel) Reid of the Royal Engineers, is given as

PLATE. XIV.

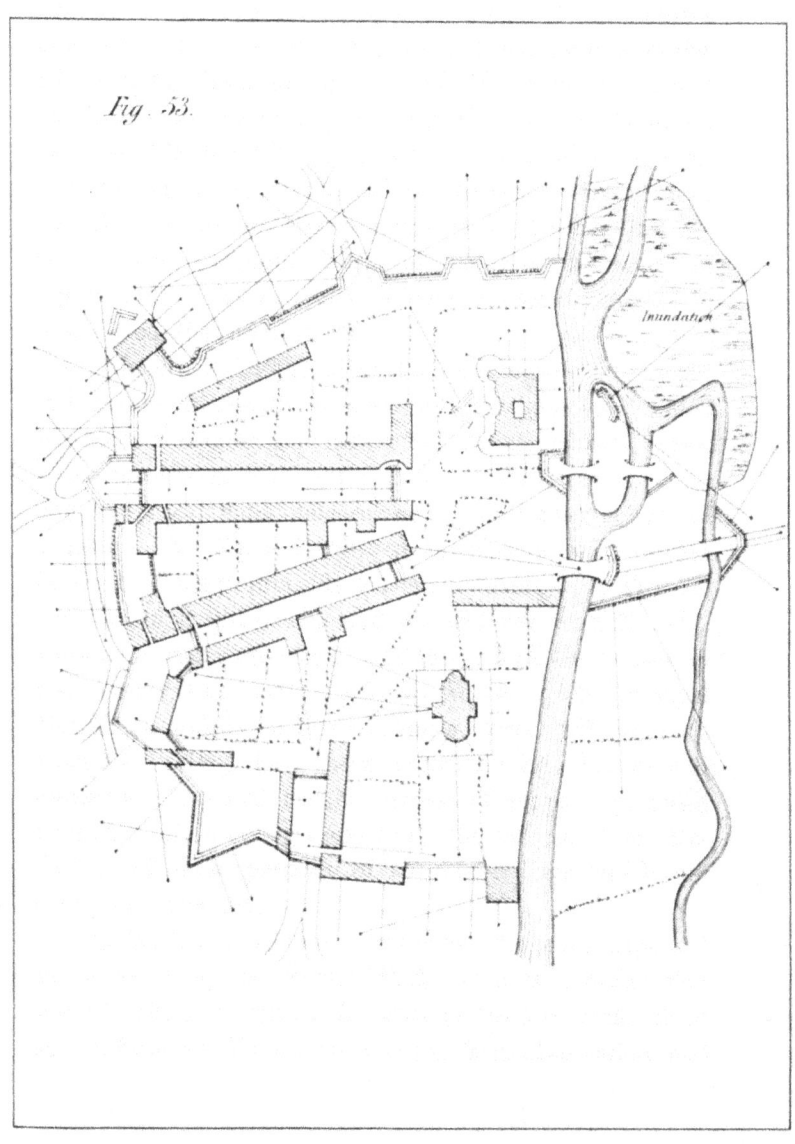

Fig. 53.

an example. In this sketch the existing buildings and streets, &c. that have been taken advantage of for defensive purposes, will be easily distinguished from the new works, which it has been necessary to add for a more effectual application of the principles adverted to in Nos. 12 to 14. On one side, the Village is covered by a River and an Inundation, which of themselves present a Barrier, and the Bridges which communicate with the country are shut up with temporary works of the nature explained in CHAP. VIII., so as to render it tolerably secure against an attack from that quarter.

On the other side the River, the buildings do not appear to have been disposed very favourably for the defence, which has made it necessary to construct a variety of new works. These have been laid out so as to give Fire to the front and reciprocal flank defence, No. 12, and they consist of Stockades, No. 75, and Earthen Breastworks with ditches in front of them, probably an improvement upon FIG. 10. The Streets it will be observed, are all Barricaded, No. 112. Communications are also broken through all the houses, in the contour close to the Parapets, No. 20. The Principal Buildings, probably a Church, and a Prison, will be easily recognised; they have been converted into Keeps, and appear well situated for the purpose of supporting, and if necessary, of receiving or covering the retreat of the Defenders of those portions of the outer lines which are contiguous to them.

120. Such works as are here treated of, are not supposed to be proof against Round Shot, which is a defect that must be charged against the want of time to make them so; if, however, Troops are secured from observation, and

from the immediate effects of Case Shot, Bullets, Sabres, and Bayonets, which are far more destructive, and that they are besides placed in an attitude to resist a superior enemy, and above all to *gain time,* it will be admitted that a great object has been attained, at a trifling expense of labour.

121. Numerous instances might be adduced where Posts, fortified in the greatest haste, have offered a more protracted and effectual resistance than more regular and more imposing Works have done; which may partly be attributed to measures of evident necessity being adopted, which might have eluded previous calculation; and to an enemy generally coming upon them unprepared with the requisite means for their attack.

The Post of Hougoumont in front of the Right Centre of the position at Waterloo, is a striking illustration not only of the importance of such Posts, but of their strength, when the Defenders are really in earnest, and determined to hold them. It possessed no advantages which might not be found in almost every substantial Farm-house and Buildings, and only a few hours' labour had been bestowed in improving them. The Duke of Wellington thus speaks of it in his Despatch to Earl Bathurst, dated Waterloo, 19th June, 1815, p. 858.

"About 10 o'clock the enemy commenced a furious attack upon our post at Hougoumont. They occupied that post with a detachment from General Byng's brigade of guards, which was in position in its rear, and it was for some time under the command of Lieut.-Colonel Macdonell, and afterwards of Colonel Home; and I am happy to add, it was maintained throughout the day with the utmost gallantry by these brave troops, notwithstanding the repeated efforts of large bodies of the enemy to obtain possession of it.

The determined attitude that troops are enabled to maintain in such a post, may be inferred from this account; and the following anecdote will show that the confidence which reigns within a post is infectious.

Late in the day, the Prince of Orange sent directions by the Earl of March,* that the wood in front of Hougoumont, which was occupied by a detachment of the Guards, should be held to the last. Lord Saltoun, who received the message, had a fine opportunity of serving up a few flowers of speech in his reply, but posterity has lost the benefit of any more elaborate record of the resolutions he formed, than is contained in the following pithy answer: " Tell him it's all right," said he.

It will ever be found that a man of energy and resource will do more for himself in a case of emergency than a man of rule; and it will be encouraging to a young Officer to reflect, that in strengthening an outpost, zeal and intelligence, aided by a very little practical knowledge, will go far to accomplish all that could be expected from scientific acquirement and greater experience.

---

* The present Duke of Richmond.

CHAP. VIII.—ARRANGEMENTS FOR THE DEFENCE OF A BRIDGE.

122. The most important results may depend on holding an enemy in check, and successfully disputing the Passage of a Bridge; it would therefore be desirable to construct Works of some extent, and of a respectable description for such a purpose. Exigencies will however occur in the Field, when this cannot be done, and it is contemplated that the duty of strengthening such a Post may devolve on an Officer in command of a Piquet. It may be useful therefore to consider what can be effected by five or six hours of active exertion applied in throwing up Temporary Works of the nature before described, under certain conditions.

123. In deciding on the general plan for the Defence of a Bridge, reference must be had to the circumstances of the contending parties, and the particular object that is to be fulfilled. For instance, if a body of Troops had to retire over a Bridge in presence of a Superior Force, Works would naturally be thrown up *in front* of it, for covering the Retreat, and ensuring its being held until the passage had been effected, and others might perhaps be placed *in rear* of it for giving Support, and prolonging the resistance; or if the protection of the Bridge itself were the object, the same plan would be followed; but if it were merely for disputing the Passage, in order to cover a Line of Operations or a Flank march, when it either could not be destroyed, or it were desirable to preserve it, Works *in*

PLATE.XV.

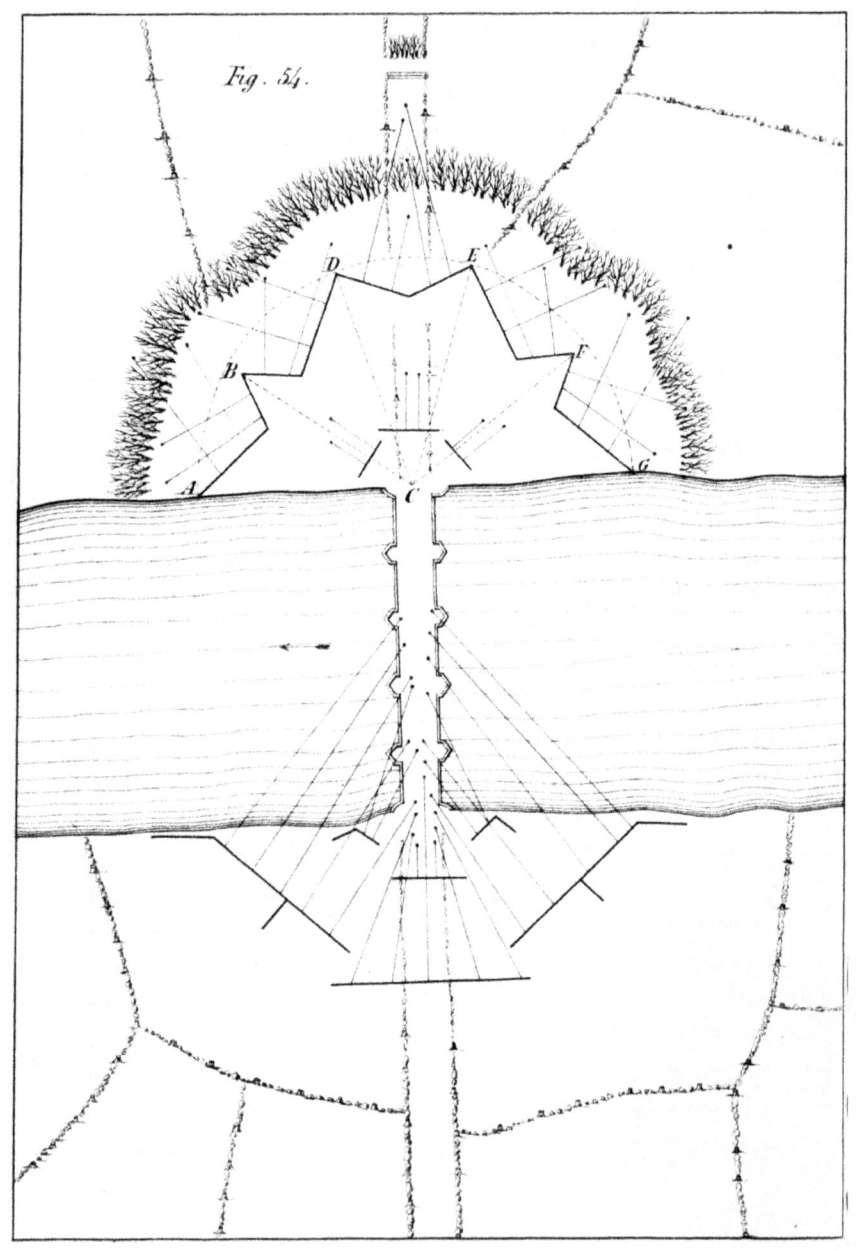

Fig. 54.

front of the Bridge would not in this case be so necessary, and it would entirely depend upon circumstances, and the relative strength of the force charged with that duty, whether the principal Works would not be more judiciously placed *in the rear*, which is obviously the most advantageous position for purely defensive purposes.

124. For the sake of illustration, it may perhaps convey a better idea of the thing, to suppose a larger Force to be employed, and more extensive Works to be undertaken, than a young Officer would be responsible for, in order that the General Principles may be more apparent; for in proportion as an Officer comprehends *all* that is going on, will be the interest he will take in any portion confided to his superintendence; and his sphere of usefulness will always keep pace with his acquirements. On most occasions it is quite as well for a Soldier not to be *thinking*, when he ought to be *obeying*, but here the two will work very well together, and at times also, it is agreeable to know the design and object of one's exertions.

125. The annexed Sketch, Fig. 54, may serve as an example of Temporary Works, thrown up in front as well as in the rear of a Bridge in an open country, for guarding it, and disputing the Passage, with a Force of 600 men available for throwing them up, and afterwards defending them; but without Artillery.

126. With a view of ascertaining in the first instance what extent of Works should be undertaken, and where they should be placed, an Officer would have to consider how he could post whatever Force he might have, to the greatest advantage for securing his object. Suppose, with 600 men under his command, he determines generally, for

the protection of the Bridge, to have three-fourths of them in advance of it, and one-fourth as a Reserve in rear; and that he thinks it advisable to post a small proportion of the former number as a Support, close to the front of the Bridge, to cover the retreat of the larger body, if driven in from the outer Works. Also that he determines to have a File of men on every running yard of Breastwork *in front* of the Bridge, to be applied as circumstances require, and to post his Main Reserve in other Works *in rear*, which shall be sufficiently extensive to receive two-thirds of his number, or 400 men, if he is afterwards obliged to fall back to a more favourable position, from his opponents being too much for him; the remainder being held in reserve further off.

127. This being his general idea of defending the Post, the following distribution of 600 men would be in accordance with it, *viz.*—

> 400 men would be posted on the Outer Line in front of the Bridge.
> 50 men close to the front of the Bridge for covering a Retreat, and to act as a Support; and
> 150 men, partially occupying the Works in rear of the Bridge, as a Reserve to the whole.

Now for the extent of Works to correspond with these numbers, and what has been said of the General Plan. 400 men, at one File to every running yard of Breastwork, would require 200 yards of Breastwork on the Outer Line: and 50 men close to the head of the Bridge would require 25 yards more, making—in all 225 yards of Breastwork front of the Bridge.

128. The Extent proportioned to the numbers being thus ascertained, the next point to decide would be, the

DEFENCE OF A BRIDGE. 69

Form in which to dispose the different Lines, on the principles laid down in Nos. 26 to 42; and in reference to the nature of the ground and circumstances, so that the whole Outline should not exceed the total length it had been judged advisable to undertake.

129. A simple way of obtaining something approaching to accuracy on the ground, would be, first of all to trace a rough semi-circle with pickets, about one-sixth part less in running length* than the required Breastwork; for doing which, it would only be necessary to remember, that the distance taken in a pair of compasses for describing a semi-circle on paper, (called a radius,) is equal to the third part of the extent it describes; so that if a semi-circle which should measure 300 yards, had to be traced on the ground, or as in this instance in front of a Bridge, FIG. 54, it would readily be done by measuring 100 yards each way, from the centre of the Bridge, along the bank of the River, and then measuring from the same central point 100 yards in several other directions, as shown dotted in the Figure; C B, C D. Stakes, or as they are usually termed, Pickets, being driven at the extremities of all these measured lines, would indicate so many points in the outline of the required semi-circle.

The Salient, or outermost angles of the proposed lines of Breastwork being fixed in the outline of the semi-circle so traced, and their lengths being disposed within the

---

* It is traced in a certain proportion less, because the Breastworks which are disposed within it, at different angles, for obtaining Flank defence, &c., necessarily have a greater development (see FIG. 54); the semi-circle or polygon being as it were a base on which a series of triangles or other figures, formed by the lines, stand. The proportion of one-sixth is merely given as an average, which may produce a result near enough the truth for our present purpose.

semi-circle, in different directions, so as to flank each other, &c., the total length of the *Trace*, though it will of course vary with the different figure that may be given to the Works, will perhaps be near enough the required extent for practice.

In the present example, the outer line in front of the Bridge is not to exceed 225 yards in running length; the outline of the Semi-circle, within which to dispose the Works, would therefore be only about 188 yards, which is one-sixth part less in extent, and the *radius* or length to be measured for describing it, will be one-third part of that distance, or 63 yards nearly; which being marked out in several directions as already explained, C A, C B, &c., would determine the points required; and when a sufficient number of them were obtained, the intermediate ones might be picketed by the eye. If from the nature of the ground the Works could not judiciously be disposed in any regular form, the semi-circle would not of course apply, but the *Principle* would. In such a case the measured distances between the most Salient points ought, of course, to be of *less extent* than the required length of Breastwork, for the reasons already stated.

130. In rear of the Bridge, we suppose that an extent of Breastwork to cover 400 men would be required (which we may estimate at 200 yards in running length); the remainder of the original number being held in reserve, further off, to act according to circumstances. This might be traced on the ground in the manner already described, but in arranging the Plan, it would have to be borne in mind that the Bridge affords the only accessible point of attack; the Works should therefore be so laid out, as that

the whole Fire should be *concentrated* upon it. It would likewise be necessary to guard against an Enfilade fire of artillery, which would be effected, either by so disposing the Lines, as that their prolongations should fall in such places on the other side the river, as were inaccessible to guns; or if that were impracticable, it would be necessary to erect substantial high Traverses at the extremities, and at intervals along the Lines subject to the Enfilade. No. 11. These Traverses may be merely short portions of Breastwork, standing perpendicular to the General Line, and made of the requisite height and thickness, to answer the purpose.

131. The Extent of Breastwork, and the position of the most Salient posts being thus determined, the Lines to connect them may be traced with sufficient accuracy by the eye. In this example the Salients are only about 40 yards apart, and it is rather a refinement breaking the Lines into smaller portions, but it serves better to explain the principle on which such Works are laid out. The Breastwork connecting these points has therefore been traced in an indented form, the advantages of which are, that in the centre portion, a more powerful Fire is directed on the most accessible part of the Abattis in front; and as regards the two sides of the Intrenchment, the Lines are not subject to be enfiladed by artillery placed at a distance on the road, which being the position most easy of access, would probably be that which Guns would occcupy in supporting an attack. A Flanking Fire is also obtained for the defence of the Salients, and a more concentrated Fire can be brought upon particular points of the Abattis, if necessary.

GENERAL PLAN AND DETAILS

132. At any convenient distance, varying from 20 to 40 or 50 yards to the front, an Abattis, or other Obstruction, is designed, parallel to the general contour of the Works, and extending to the River on each side. There is no necessity for its being of any regular form, so that it is connected; and in executing it, advantage would of course be taken of all Fences or local facilities that might offer.

133. The Details of executing all this Work now remain to be considered. There are supposed to be 225 yards of Breastwork in front, and 200 yards in rear of the Bridge, altogether 425 yards; which, at 2 yards a man, would require 212 men for working on it. If this arrangement were adopted, it would leave 388 men disposable for making the abattis in front,—pulling down the parapet Walls, in order to lay any Force passing the Bridge under the Fire of the Defenders,—making Barricades across the Bridge,—blocking up the Roads, and other necessary Works; or if the Working Parties at the Breastworks, had a yard and a half in length to execute, instead of 2 yards, 283 men would be employed on the Breastworks, and 317 would remain disposable;—or if the Obstructions were already in existence, in the shape of Hedges, Drains, &c., the Breastworks might be double manned, and the men extended at work, as explained in No. 53; circumstances would decide which arrangement was the best. The Profile to be given to these Works, would be regulated by the considerations adverted to in CHAP. III. A reference also to FIGS. 2 and 3, will show that the most accessible points, should have a different Profile from those which are not open to attack, and which only afford *cover* for Troops. For instance, in front of the Bridge, all the

FOR THE DEFENCE OF A BRIDGE. 73

Works should offer the greatest possible impediment to an Assault, and therefore the Profiles should be of the nature described in No. 56; but in rear of the Bridge, the Breastworks close to the front of it should be made from a Trench, Figs. 4 to 8, which in merely affording Cover for the Defenders, should, when taken, leave the Assailants as much exposed as possible to the Fire of the more extensive Works behind them; and these again should be made of the Profile adopted in front of the Bridge for the reasons stated.

134. If the Force of disputing the passage of a Bridge were very much smaller than is here assumed, no difficulty would be found in executing works of an extent to correspond, that would offer rather more than a proportionate resistance. Supposing there were only 50 men, or less than that, for working and defence, a good Breastwork with an Abattis before it, or a deep cut with Pallisades, &c., No. 144, might be made across the Bridge, close to the front, another such Barricade might be added in the centre, and a third at the foot* of a Bridge, flanked by short Breastworks along the river side, where a final stand would be made. It would be necessary to look out that there was no Ford near, and no swimming over on rafts going on, and a handful of Defenders would then be very respectably off. Care would also be taken to secure them from the effects of Artillery, by digging out a good Trench for cover, and by making the Parapets as thick as circumstances permitted; such materials also should be used for

---

* The Head and Foot of a Bridge are synonymous with the front and rear of it, considered with reference to the direction in which Troops are defending it.

the Parapets as do not splinter when struck by shot, for it must be remembered that the limited front of a Barricade, would cause the whole fire to be concentrated upon it; and any thing that would tend to lessen its effect, would be deserving of attention. If Stones necessarily formed the mass which was raised, they should as much as possible, be covered up with earth, mud, brushwood, &c. With a still smaller Force, as already hinted, it might be desirable to confine the defence to the foot of the Bridge; the side walls would, in that case, be removed, so as to expose an attacking Force at any flank fire that could be brought to bear; the road way would be as much encumbered with the materials or other obstructions as possible; which with a good Barricade, obstinately defended, would render an attack rather a hazardous and difficult operation.

135. Similar principles and details to those laid down for strengthening a Village, No. 114, would be applicable to a Bridge, if the ends of it were closed in by Buildings; Obstacles, and Barricades, in successive lines, with Flanking Fire from the Houses on each side, and *plenty of it*.

The duty of "Watching a Ford," with a view to dispute any attempt of an enemy to avail himself of it, would be fulfilled in following out the same principles, as far as they would apply; and all the details would of course correspond with the specific objects that were to be attained. The defence however would, in almost all cases, be confined to the *safe side* of the river; for the Ford must be a very good Ford indeed, that did not present something of an obstacle in itself, or at least the facility of creating one, by some of the temporary expedients adverted to in Nos. 81 to 83; and nobody would choose to sacrifice these advan-

DEFENCE OF A FORD.

tages for the satisfaction of engaging an enemy under less favourable circumstances. It would be prudent therefore to keep the Ford *in front,* and make the best of it. In a narrow river, and with a little assistance from *good luck*, it might be possible to add a little to the depth of water at a Ford; and it must not be forgotten, that even a few inches, especially in a rapid current, might be *worth having.* It might make a difference of swamping the Pouches of the Assailants, or sweeping some of them off their legs, and creating confusion. It will not do to talk of the construction of a Dam, for that sounds beyond our means, and as if we were trenching upon the privileges of Engineers: but any temporary obstacle which arrests a stream, has the effect of holding water up, and, if opportunity offers, a few Trees felled across, or dragged into any situation below a Ford, will form a base for the further operation of adding any stray Gates, Hurdles, Brushwood, Sods, and Rubbish that come to hand; and in proportion to the Time and Labour that may be judiciously bestowed, will, even this, be found *better than nothing.*

CHAP. IX.—DEFENCE OF AN INTRENCHMENT.

136. It is hoped that the foregoing pages may have shown that there is no great difficulty in fortifying an Outpost with various Temporary Works, that shall give Cover and protection to the Defenders of them, and that a little knowledge, which is said to be a "dangerous thing" on most other subjects, will suffice for this. The DEFENCE OF AN INTRENCHMENT, when it is made, is however perhaps a more difficult affair, and it may not be considered out of place briefly to advert to it, with a view of pointing out some of its leading features, and wherein it differs from the ordinary routine of Service in the Field.

The general dispositions for the defence of an Intrenchment, are the same in *principle* as those of a Force acting on the Defensive, in an Open position; in both cases a Line is formed for resisting an attack, and this Line being forced, is a prelude to defeat; in either case the *fighting men* must be sustained by a Reserve, &c.; but as the Force for the defence of an Intrenchment is not in a situation for manœuvring so freely as in the Field, and are thus deprived of a powerful means of remedying any partial success of an enemy, by change of position, it becomes the more essential that all measures which will tend to instil *Confidence*, should be adopted and persevered in. If the truth of this remark is not disputed, it would appear that *Support* is more necessary to a man engaged in repelling the attack of a Breastwork, than in the open field. Again, under the latter circumstances his resistance is of a more passive character. The crossing of bayonets, and maintaining a personal combat, is comparatively of rare occurrence; but the defence of a Parapet is altogether another thing, every man must be a "fire eater" whether he will or no, if he does his duty; for anything approaching the character of a vigorous defence, may only be said to *begin* when an Enemy is within arm's length. If the very ground you stand upon is yielded for an inch, your object is in a great measure defeated; for it is far safer to keep people out of a work by determined resistance, than to let them make good their footing, and trust to the chance of expelling them by assuming the offensive.

It will be obvious, however, that no particular rules can be advanced to meet all circumstances, but a Commander is responsible for adapting General Principles to every exigency that may arise on Service; and as before said, it is only by knowing what special objects he has to attain, and what dispositions will best conduce to secure them, that he will be enabled to act with decision and effect.

137. For the sake of illustration, we will assume that a Road leading through a defile to the Flanks of a Position, has been shut up by an Intrenched Line of a decent profile;—that it is in a state to be defended, and that 600 Men and two Field pieces have been detached for occupying it, with orders to hold an Enemy in check as long as possible, without compromising their own safety; and that they are to be left to their own resources to make the best of it. Further, that the Flanks of the Intrenchment are secured by the nature of the ground, and that therefore, when an Assault is made, it will be "a fair stand up fight."

It would perhaps not be amiss under such circumstances,

to man the Breastworks with one-half the Force, and hold the other half, as a Reserve and Supports. 300 men would therefore on this supposition be disposed along the interior of the different lines of Breastwork; one-half of the remainder, or 150 men, might be brought up in either Column or Line, as appeared best, about 100 yards in rear, opposite the weakest point, and with free communication to the Front, and the remaining 150 might be posted further off as a Reserve, to act according to circumstances. The two guns would be placed so as to see an advancing Column at the greatest distance, and in a position to do it the greatest damage as it came up. Every facility for retiring should be looked to, and a fresh point should previously be selected where the Guns might be posted for covering a Retreat, if the Works were carried, or for supporting the advance of the Reserve, when charging the Assailants, to regain possession of them. Each Officer and Man should have his exact Post assigned to him, and be thoroughly instructed in the Duties that would be required of him, under the different circumstances of Attack that might be foreseen. It would be explained to the men posted for the Defence of the Parapet, what was the particular object of each Line, and to what they must direct their attention. How they could best cover themselves when giving their Fire; when was the most favourable time for Charging the Assailants, and what was to be done if they beat them off. What would be the line of Retreat, and the point of reforming, if the Works were forced: what was to be done for regaining possession of them, &c. The conduct to be observed by the Supports, the Reserve, and the Artillery, in these circumstances, would likewise be clearly laid down, and the whole Force should be made to appreciate the strength of the Work, the many advantages they possessed over their Assailants, and the best way of profiting by them.

When the nature of the Attack was sufficiently defined, the general dispositions that had been made to meet it, might be modified so as to correspond. Thus the men defending the Parapets would be closed in on those Lines that flanked the approaching Columns, and towards the threatened point, where, besides those who were giving their Fire over the top of the Parapet, others would be drawn up close in rear of them for giving instant Support, &c. These men would also be advantageously employed in loading for the Files in front, for in order to maintain a very vigorous Fire, the men for defending a Parapet should be drawn up four deep. The best and steadiest shots should be selected to line the Parapet, at the distance of about a yard, or a little more apart, which will enable them to cover themselves, and give their fire with freedom, and the rear files have then nothing to do, but to load and relieve those in front in succession, should the firing be kept up for any length of time. By this arrangement each man in front might fire 50 rounds in five minutes, taking a steady aim, when if he had to load for himself, he could not Fire more than about 15 rounds, which is sufficient proof of the advantage which is gained.*

When these dispositions were made, all that would remain to be done, would be, to stop the head of the assaulting

---

* Philippon, at Badajos, adopted something like this mode, and it was practised with murderous effect at New Orleans.

column, by a determined and obstinate resistance at the Parapet; failing in this, to make an instant and vigorous Charge with the Supports, whilst the Enemy was reforming and in confusion within the Work; or if the worst came to the worst, to effect a steady and orderly Retreat, should these good intentions have been frustrated. Columns of Assault, and Storming Parties, are sometimes so very unreasonable, they will not be denied, and when that is the case they may get into a Work, but they ought at least *to pay a good price for it;* and they generally have done so, when anything worthy the name of a Defence has been made.

138. It will be admitted from the foregoing observations, that in the Defence of Works, *much more* is expected from individual exertion and personal bravery, than in the Open Field, where there may be plenty of fighting without absolute contact, and where change of position and tactic, save an infinity of trouble. A Soldier therefore, in these encounters, becomes much less of a warlike machine, than under circumstances when he is more usually content to play at *long shot,* and see all opposition vanish in a moment as he rushes forward at the word "Charge," and long before he has an opportunity of measuring the length of his Bayonet with his opponent. It is therefore but reasonable to suppose, that these important duties cannot be performed with all the advantages which are within the influence of Instruction to impart, unless a Soldier were made thoroughly to comprehend all he had to do, and the best mode of doing it, and that his *morale* were cultivated in proportion to the exertions required.

139. It is too much to expect that a little Field Work,

of an inconsiderable profile, will enable men to perform such miracles, as they could under more imposing circumstances; all that is necessary to impress is, that *much is to be done* and that *much may be done;* and, that the Defence of a Parapet, is a very different thing from sustaining a Charge in an Open position. There is far more to be done,—more energy is required,—more individual exertion, and courage. In fact, a good Defence becomes like a Fight of olden times, when two-handed Swords and ponderous Battle Axes were wielded by the brawny arms of our Saxon and Norman forefathers; when such fellows as "Reginald front de Bœuf," ate the plum pudding of England;—fellows who, in the ordinary course of their morning's amusement, would give and take blows for half an hour, every one of which would have annihilated a rhinoceros. Those were the men that learnt the style of fighting best adapted for an obstinate defence: the Field Exercise, as doubtless then taught in the Drill Squads of those days, would have made them stand to their work at a Parapet, as a Blacksmith does at his Anvil, milling away "right merrilie" at the thick skulls of their adversaries; nor is it doubted for a moment, that their Successors, of modern times, the present Malt-consuming Army of England, have all the will and Heart to do the same, were they equally instructed, and had better tools to work with. But the instinctive hardihood of the British Soldier, is perhaps, after all, his best Drill-master, when he gets within reach of his Adversary; it may however be *hinted*, without disparagement to a Firelock, that it is not a Weapon, of all others, one would choose for a combat of personal strength and address at close quarters, into which all Assaults and

Defences, more or less, resolve themselves, when there are serious intentions enlisted on both sides: this however forms the exception to its general usefulness for other purposes, and necessity almost forbids any other being thought of, or suggested, in addition, to meet remote exigencies of the service. On such *grand* occasions as the regular defence of Breaches, &c., a variety of Weapons, chiefly very long ones, are sometimes paraded, but let that pass as foreign to the present subject, and let us trust to our Bayonets, as there is no help for it: they have hitherto accomplished Deeds that make one's hair stand on end to think of, in these Piping times of Peace; and, instead of being cried down, they ought to be crowned with a portion of the same Laurels that adorn the brows of the Heroes who have either directed, or used them.

Chap. X.—Guarding and Defending a House.

140. Having explained in Chap. VI. some of the means for placing a House in a state to be defended, a few observations respecting the disposal of Defenders may perhaps be of use. When the Defences were in a state to be occupied, a Commander would, under most circumstances, divide his Force into as many Parties as there were distinct portions of works to be occupied. For example, one Party for each Story, No. 90, one for an Outhouse, another for the Stables, &c., their numbers corresponding with the extent of the Works they were to defend. He would explain to each Officer, or Non-commissioned Officer in command of these portions, how their duties were to be performed, what object they had to fulfil, and what was to be expected from them;—when was the proper time for opening a Musketry fire from the Loop-holes;—when the critical moment for dipping a Rocket into an advancing Column;—when the throwing of Grenades should commence, or small Shells be rolled down. How the different Communications were arranged from the Out-buildings to the House, and from one Story to another. What means had been provided for closing these Communications, and under what circumstances a retreat should be made to the Upper floors, if the Post were to be defended to the last, or elsewhere if it should become necessary to abandon it.

The Parties might then be told off by their own Commanders to specific duties. For example, two men to each Loop-hole in exposed situations, and one to all others, who would also be disposable for *double manning* those on the sides attacked; or this might be done, if more convenient, from the Reserve. In the Lower story and Outworks a greater proportion would be posted than in the Upper stories, which are not so liable to be forced. A special Guard would be placed at all Doors or Lower Windows open to assault, and a small Reserve would be held in readiness, especially on the Ground floor, to act according to circumstances; for reinforcing particular situations when pressed, or if a Barricade were forced, for charging the Assailants, or covering the Retreat of the Defenders, to those points they had been ordered to retire upon. Other men would be held in readiness to make use of the means provided for cutting off the Communications, No. 99, or to stop up any partial breach that might have been made by artillery, either through the Walls or Barricades. The situations to which men might retire for Cover against artillery fire until their services were required, might also be pointed out, &c.

141. If after an obstinate resistance an Enemy should drive the Defenders from all their strongholds below, it would be remembered that the Upper story was their Citadel; and it will be obvious that with a barricaded Staircase, they would be in a position from which they could not be very easily dislodged, if they were determined to hold it. Without refining however, too much on the Defence, and leaving Hot Water, Quick Lime, Molten Lead, and a host of *small fry* which have been recommended as accessaries on such an occasion, to those who have leisure to prepare and make use of them, Attention is merely invited to the Fact, that a Hole here and there

through an Upper floor, would give passage to as many Grenades, as of themselves would make it very lively work in the Lower regions; and that a few additional ones for Musketry, would afford the means of adding to any confusion that might result. The attempt to force a well barricaded Staircase, so as to gain access to the Upper stories, would always be a hazardous operation, and here the advantage is manifestly on the side of the Defence; but we may not feel too secure in these good quarters, for it must be admitted that there would be little difficulty in the Assailants setting fire to the House, or in making arrangements for blowing it up, which, under most circumstances, it might be prudent to receive as a formal " *Notice to quit.*"

CHAP. XI.—GUARDING AND DEFENDING AN INTRENCHED VILLAGE.

142. The general disposition of a Force for the Defence of an Intrenched Village, would be influenced by the principles adverted to in CHAP. IX, as far as the difference of locality and circumstances will permit of their application; and as the chief Defensive Works would usually consist of a combination of Buildings and Intrenchments, &c., which have been separately under consideration in the preceding pages, it will be needless again to enter into the *Local* disposition of the Defenders of such Works, or the means to which they should resort, for resisting an Attack. A Village however may be of considerable extent, calling for additional precautions and defensive measures, corresponding to its importance as a Military Post: a few further remarks on the subject may therefore not be superfluous, as they may at least serve to combine under one general plan, the separate Defences of such detached portions as would be under the superintendence of individual Officers, and thus render each part more intelligible.

143. To guard against a Surprise, and to be in readiness to repel an attack at any moment, and in any quarter, are objects demanding equal attention, and are the mainspring and basis of all Defensive measures. The former of these important points will be secured by an adherence to those golden rules which appear in Sect. 8, Part V., of the Field Exercise, in which the Duties of advanced Picquets, and their Sentries, Patrols, &c., are clearly laid down and ex-

plained; the latter by judicious internal arrangements, in occupying the different Works to advantage,—posting the Picquets, Reserve, and Support, so as to enable them to do their Duties with decision and effect,—appointing convenient situations for assembly on the first alarm,—judiciously quartering the Troops, &c.

144. In making these preliminary arrangements for the Defence, a Commander would never lose sight of the great importance of getting every man to his Post in the least possible time; and when he had ascertained by false alarms or other means, what he could trust to in that respect, his next care would be to take such steps, as would at least insure sufficient notice of the approach of an Enemy, to enable him to dispose of his Force without hurry, for giving him a warm reception. For instance, it might require half an hour to do this leisurely, and he would therefore, on this supposition, so distribute his Outposts, &c., as to feel secure of having that time to himself, after the first alarm was given, and before an Attack could possibly be made. If he fails in having sufficient notice to do this, it is 10 to 1 he is beat, for the best measures will be of little avail, if they cannot be carried into full effect. It will be needless to harass Troops by multiplying Outposts so as to secure earlier intelligence than is required, but still it will be an error on the right side to take 20 precautions too many, rather than to neglect a single one. In making his dispositions therefore, he would endeavour to steer a middle course between two extremes; on the one hand, if Troops are overworked in preparing for an Attack, and guarding against a Surprise, they are thrown out of condition for resisting it when made,—on the other, if all due precautions

are not taken for first strengthening the Post, and then guarding it, they risk the loss of all their labour in being exposed to a sudden Attack, at a time when they are in no form for opposing adequate resistance.

In the distribution of the Defenders too, there are extremes to be avoided; for instance,—if all the Parapets and Works are manned without regard to the requisite Force which should be in reserve for giving Support, though the greater number formed for opposing a first shock might lessen the danger of being upset by it, yet a Line cannot stand up for any length of time against a Column, that from circumstances can be brought into contact with it; and when once it is forced at two or three points, the game is pretty nearly up, unless there is something fresh to go to work with. The opposite defect would be in giving undue strength to the Reserve at the expense of the Parapets, which from being feebly defended, would not then offer the resistance they ought to oppose. Another such a Scylla and Charybdis, and another to that, might be added if these little principles were pursued further, but we may safely trust to common sense suggesting more on the spot, under the ever-varying circumstances that arise on Service than the *memory* can supply,—provided that the *simple Principles* and *Essentials* of the subject have made that impression on the mind, which has secured their *saliency*. If they are *at home* when wanted, there is a natural tendency in minor matters to fall into their places and come right of themselves, and we will therefore leave the rough outline as it is.

145. The proportion of the disposable Force to be retained in hand for the Reserve, would be governed by cir-

cumstances, depending on the number of assailable points, and the calls that might be expected to be made upon it for assistance,—perhaps from one-fourth to one-sixth of the whole would not be far off the mark. The remainder would be subdivided for a variety of duties, such as a Garrison for each separate House that had been strengthened, and one for the Keep,—Defenders for the Intrenchments, Breastworks, and Stockades,—Picquets, Guards, &c.

146. A strong Reserve Picquet should be mounted at the rallying point of the Reserve, which should be near the centre of the Village, in some open place having free communication to all the Defences. Another Picquet would be in the Keep, and according to circumstances others might be required at different points. An outlying Picquet or two would be equally necessary in commanding situations beyond the Works, and a communication between all of them should be kept up by a chain of Sentries, or frequent patrolling. If Cavalry form part of the Force, some of the Outpost duties during the daytime should be intrusted to them, as they can patrol to a greater distance to see what is going on, and obtain information. In the evening they would be replaced by Infantry, but if the Posts were distant, a few Cavalry patrols should be attached, to assist in keeping up the communication, or to gallop in with intelligence. The Picquets would of course be accoutred and ready to stand to their arms at an instant's warning, and those for the immediate defence of any distinct portion of the Works, such as Intrenchments or Barricades, should either be hutted or encamped close to the spot, or lodged in the nearest building, if one were found conveniently situated for the purpose; this is essential, for an Enemy if un-

opposed for even a few minutes, will surmount without difficulty such Obstacles as are usually met with in the temporary Works that have been treated of.

147. Every Commanding Officer of a Regiment should have a steady Non-commissioned Officer of each Company to sleep within hail of him every night;—one who is perfectly acquainted with the quarters of every Officer and Non-commissioned Officer in his Company; so that at any instant, orders might be conveyed with the utmost promptitude to any part of the Corps, however much it might be distributed. And on the same principle, every Officer in Command of a Company which was detached, should retain the means of readily communicating orders.

The Support too, should be close at hand in the nearest houses, and they should have a hint that there is no necessity for being *shy* about breaking out fresh doors, or doing anything else, that may make their Communications more *direct* or *convenient*. On these occasions it should always be borne in mind that a *straight* road is the shortest, and if it is a *wide* one so much the better, provided it is not one that an Enemy can avail himself of. In more permanent Works, there is not this extreme necessity for having the Defenders of them as it were, constantly under arms to repel an Attack; for if a sharp look-out is kept, the Obstacles presented by deep and wide Ditches, stout Palisading, &c., will of themselves, consume as much time of the Assailants, as will enable the Defenders to repair to their Posts, even if it were at rather shorter notice than might be agreeable; but here it is obviously a matter of paramount necessity.

AN INTRENCHED VILLAGE. 91

These precautions having been taken for guarding a Village against a Surprise, and for immediate Defence, and the remainder of the Force being apportioned according to circumstances for occupying the different Works and Buildings, it would become an object to quarter them all as close as might be, to the scene of their exertions, that there should be no unnecessary delay in getting them to their Posts, No. 144. Each separate Detachment should have a Sentry to stir them up on the first alarm, and when circumstances required it, they should all sleep on their Arms, or they will not make so quick "a turn out" of it as may be wanted. Every precaution should be multiplied by 2, when the nights are dark and tempestuous, as that is "the time o' day" for a Surprise. During the winter too, when men cannot be so much exposed Under Arms, and human nature is prone to look for scraps of creature comfort, under the lee of anything that will protect them from a keen North-Easter, the attention of Officers cannot be too much directed to enforce these Duties, and to see that every body who ought to be on the alert is so. A single Sentry standing with his back up behind a Tree, or under a Parapet, instead of snuffing the morning air with his face the other way, might cause the sacrifice of the whole Post. Indeed when all has been done that the most zealous watchfulness could dictate, a Commander and most of his people should still "sleep with one eye open" if the enemy is within a march of him. The best measures that can be devised are not infallible, even by day, and to prevent being *taken short* at night, it is safest to consider that a Column of Attack, with Grenadier Caps and Mustachios, all teeth, hair and steel, might rise up out of the bowels of the earth, or drop from the clouds, close in front of the Defences at any moment. If you are prepared for such emergencies as these, you may go to bed with the conviction that you are ready for him; and let an Enemy then do his worst, you will at least have the satisfaction of not having been outwitted.

148. Among other things, it is most essential that every Officer and Soldier should be thoroughly instructed in the nature of the Work he had to defend, and the Duties he had to perform, in all the exigencies which prudence could foresee. They should also be perfectly acquainted with every street, alley, or footpath by which they might have to move, so that on the first alarm, even if the night were as dark as pitch, there would be no confusion or mistake in repairing to their respective alarm-posts, and afterwards being posted for the Defence according to whatever orders might have been given.

149. If it should seem desirable, and the Garrison is sufficiently strong to afford to make a Sortie, it is essential that it should be well-timed and vigorously executed, and be in sufficient force to make some impression, either as a diversion in favour of the Defenders of the Parapet, or to drive the Assailants back beyond the Obstacles they may have already surmounted. The Party may be selected from the Reserve and the Defenders of the interior of the Village, leaving the Parapets fully manned, as they ought to be. The Sorties should be drawn up at the points by which they are to go out, and at the critical moment when the speed of the Assailants has been first checked by the opposition they might meet with in front, a furious onset with the Bayonet should be made on one or both Flanks, and

when the object was effected, the Troops should retire within the Works again, as fast as they came out. The Firing from the Defences would cease whilst they were engaged, and be resumed with the utmost vigour, the moment the Front was clear again. Arrangements should also be made for covering their Retreat, by being in readiness on the neighbouring Parapets to open a heavy Fire the instant it was required.

150. During an Attack, the Reserve should be within ear shot of the Commander of the Post or his Bugle, as it would be by the instantaneous application of this part of the Force at the right moment, that his hopes of remedying any disaster would mainly depend.

Before he determines to strike a decisive blow with so important abody, a Commander should assure himself that the Attack is a *real* one, and that the Defenders and their Support have been unable to deal with it; and when he has made up his mind to fire this his *great Gun*, he should bring forward the whole, or a portion of the Force to the spot, as might seem expedient, and make the most impetuous Attack possible; for if the Reserve is checked, and the original Defenders of the Work are still in disorder, it will be up-hill work to regain the ascendancy. But however desperate the case might become, it would be as well, just to try one's luck, and "have another shy at them," for the local knowledge of the Defenders gives them immense advantages, No. 20. The whole Force should rally, and be re-formed at some little distance, and a desperate Attack be directed on the Front and Flanks of the Assailants, who we may reasonably conclude would not be in the very best order for receiving it;—and if it were successful, and they were fairly driven back, all would be right again. The Reserve would regain its Post, the Defenders and the Support would do the same, and everything would then be ready for another round.

If, however, a Commander sees that it "won't do," and that he is overmatched either by the combinations or numbers of his Enemy, it remains for him to conform to circumstances.

151. It is stated in No. 110, that Villages may be intrenched under different circumstances, the chief of which are,—whether the Force defending them is to be supported from the Flanks or Rear during an Attack, or whether the Post is to be considered independent of other operations, and therefore to be defended to the last by the Troops thrown into it. In the former case, the communication with the Rear and on the Flanks, and the means of holding the ground by a succession of defensive Lines, would have been previously arranged, which would give the supporting Troops the opportunity of acting with effect, whilst the original Force was reforming. In the latter, a Keep would have been indispensable, and the Reserve would protect the Retreat of the different Detachments from the more open Works of the Contour into this stronghold, where they might be more safely indulged in showing fight, after the manner prescribed in CHAP. X.

Much however would have to be done on both sides before a retreat to the Keep or anywhere else would be thought of; and as *much* cannot be done without an expenditure of *Time* to do it in, the object of defending the Post at all, might still be fulfilled, whatever the issue of the combat might be; for in all combined operations we may say with a French author, "*Que le But de l'Art Defensif est de gagner du Temps.*"

More important ends than saving a little time are however frequently gained at the trifling cost of taking the trouble to strengthen a Post; for the determined attitude which all the Troops affected by the operation are enabled to assume from feeling a proper confidence in the resources which may be acquired by these means, either for defending themselves, or for repelling an attack, may have the effect of warding off a threatened blow altogether. There is certainly something in the bristling look of an Abattis, and the mischievous aspect of a Wall or building full of Loopholes, enlivened by an occasional peep at a Cap or a Bayonet, that is more calculated to induce a little reflection than when dangers are more obviously inviting; and when people once begin to reflect, they may think *twice* about the matter,—*second* thoughts are sometimes best.

In illustration of these remarks, and of the subject generally which has been treated of in these pages, we will wind up after the manner of other Elementary Writers, by an *Example*, only that it shall be a *real* one, of measures which have been actually pursued in converting a House and its appliances into a small Fortress, and of the effect which this hasty creation assisted in producing.

152. After the Duke of Wellington passed the Pyrenees, the French Army continued to hold Bayonne, which being situated at the junction of the Nive with the Adour, commanded the passage of both Rivers. The Allied Army had its Right beyond the Nive, whilst its centre was separated from its Left by some very marshy ground. In front of the Central position were three Buildings; on the right stood

the Château of Arcanques, in the centre a Church of the same name, and on the left, at the distance of about 300 yards, there was a large Farm House;—all three were barricaded and occupied.

It would lead us far beyond our limits to detail the advantages resulting to a position from the occupation of strong prominent points, in front of a posted Force, especially when they are drawn up on the defensive;* we will therefore say no more on the General Principles of such a measure, but confine ourselves to the details of strengthening the Château,—for the outlines of which we are indebted to the distinguished Officer who executed them.

The Château was built of stone, and was what we should call a modern, substantial, square House. One can fancy what George Robins would have said of its Groves and Avenues, and fruitful Gardens, &c.; though we dare not emulate his beguiling eloquence. We can imagine also the pride of the Seigneur in the beauties of his residence, and his feelings on viewing the ruthless alterations which were made in adapting it to the purposes required: it is foreign, however, to the purpose, to be imaginative.

The side of the Château, looking towards the rear of the position, opened into a garden surrounded with a high wall, which wall was loop-holed. The Stables were on the opposite side, in front, and they served in a great measure to cover the wall of the house itself, from the best position for cannon, on what soon became the Enemy's ground. The Mangers answered for Banquettes, after the Wall above them was loop-holed. But these Stable Walls were

---

* See No. 117.

THE CHATEAU OF ARCANQUES. 97

not so thick as those of the House, and as it did not appear likely that they would resist the first cannon shot, preparations were made to set them on fire at the moment the Enemy's Infantry should attack; for had they got into them, they probably would have found Loop-holes in the rear, through which to fire against the main Building, all ready made by their own shot.

A Grove of old Elms helped in like manner to cover the Garden Wall from the Enemy's best position for Cannon, and only a portion of these were in consequence cut down to be converted into Abbatis, &c.

The Stables were afterwards connected with the main Building by means of an Intrenchment, with a Ditch in its front. This Intrenchment was crowned with Loopholes, made with blocks, cut off with a cross-cut saw from the large elm trees, which were intended to be removed during a Cannonade, and replaced just before the assault. The Earth of which the Parapet was formed, was allowed to roll to its own natural slope; that is, it was not levelled at the top, as is usually done, under the idea of gaining thickness, but it was left as a rough triangle, in order to procure the greatest possible Command, as well as the greatest possible Cover from the Enemy's close Musketry Fire at the moment of attacking the Work; in fact it was much the same as the Parapet of a Siege Trench, and like it had its Banquette made by simply keeping a small step clear on the Interior slope.

The French General having concentrated his Forces at Bayonne in December 1813, unexpectedly and rapidly drove in the Duke of Wellington's Outposts in front of this central position; pushing on until he occupied a ridge only 500 yards in front of these barricaded Buildings, and bringing up a Field Battery, which immediately, at this short distance, opened upon them. After awhile, however, he drew off, and marching to his right, chose rather to engage the extreme left of the Allies, and on the afternoon of the same day, fought a severe action at Biaritz, and was repulsed. The French however maintaining the little ridge, 500 yards in front of the Central position, strengthened it by Loop-holeing the scattered houses of the Village, which stood within their portion of the ground; and not content with this, in the night they converted an embankment into a Battery, in which there were no less than fifteen Embrasures bearing on the Chateau. These were masked with branches of Trees, and as the position was within two leagues of Bayonne, it was thought very possible that heavy guns might have been brought up from that Fortress to arm some of them.

This consideration, however, did not alter the determination which had been made to hold and defend the Post, which shows that a House is not to be considered untenable because " the Enemy can bring cannon against it." A Battalion of the Rifle Brigade was thrown in, to garrison it, and with characteristic gallantry and activity, they made every preparation for an obstinate and vigorous resistance. Story after story was to have been disputed, by retreating upwards if it became necessary,*—the Cellar doors, and those of the Basement story were thrown open, that a portion of the Defenders might have been placed in security whilst the cannonade lasted, and until the Assault began,—

---

* See No. 141

Precautions were taken to prevent the Enemy setting fire to the House with Shells or other means,—and Serjeants were placed in the Stables with burning brands in their hands, in readiness, when the order was given, to fire the dead Brushwood, which had been collected there to accelerate their destruction. Whilst these preparatory arrangements were in progress, a movement of the British Reserve Division suddenly caused the French Army to be put under arms, and the alarm being taken up by their Opponents, both sides stood in suspense, each expecting the other's Attack. The Battery with its formidable array of Embrasures, though masked with branches, was seen to be alive, with moving heads, and nothing appeared to be wanting on either side but the signal to begin.

As the fate of the Battle might have depended on holding the Château, Major Reid of the Engineers, under whose able direction this Post hàd been strengthened, had asked and obtained his General's permission to share in the honour of its Defence; but History has doubtless been deprived of a bright page, and we of a valuable practical Example, in the opportunity being denied.

The favourable situation of the Outposts,—the strength they possessed in themselves, and that which they relatively imparted to the position, probably weighed with the French Marshal, in determining him not to risk an Attack. It may be remarked however, *en passant*, that there were close at hand, 10,000 of those Veteran Troops, whom "The Duke" "could lead any where, and with whom he "could do any thing" and all in *rare* condition for work, as they would say in Yorkshire, which doubtless formed an item in the calculation.

Be that as it may however, the Marshal did not altogether like the look of things, for on the third night of the operations he moved off, and on the morning of the fourth day evinced a preference for attacking the extreme Right of the Army which was beyond the Nive, rather than encounter the Central position, which had been hastily strengthened in the manner described.

www.ingramcontent.com/pod-product-compliance
Lightning Source LLC
Chambersburg PA
CBHW070159100426
42743CB00013B/2976